100 Snacks special (Vegetarian)

By

Mrs.S.Mallika Badrinath   B.Sc (Home Science)

"Cooking Made Easier"
"Wishful cooking made a reality"
with Books on Cookery & M.H.P Masala powders
by Mrs.S.Mallika Badrinath

Publishers & Books Sellers:

PRADEEP ENTERPRISES

No:20 (Old No:90), Poes Garden,
Chennai: 600 086. India.
Phone : 44-24990872 / 24997130
email: spradeep@vsnl.com

Price: **Rs. 60/-**

First Edition: November 1991
eighth Reprint : June 2007
@ Copy rights reserved

Photos by R.Ramanidharan

Our books on cookery:

In English:
100 Vegetarian Gravies
100 Rice Delights
100 Tiffin Varieties
100 Snacks special
100 Vegetarian Soups & Soft Drinks
100 Murukkus & Mixtures
100 Delicious Vegetarian Curries
100 Excellent Puddings
100 Chutney Varieties
100 Egg Recipes
100 Selected Pickles
100 South Indian Microwave Recipes
100 Refreshing Juices
100 Soya Foods
200 Classic Lunch Recipes
200 Traditional Sweets
300 Recipes for Diabetics
50 Electric Tawa Recipes
50 Pongal Festival Delights
25 Sweet corn Recipes

Other Books:
25 Small Fur Toys

In Telugu:
100 Masala Kurma varieteelu
100 Biriyani Rice varieteelu
100 Tiffin Varieteelu
100 Chiru Thindi varieteelu
100 Ruchigala Masala Kooralu
100 Vindhu Bojana Vantakaalu
200 Theepi Vantakaalu

In Hindi
200 Dhakshina Bharath Bhojan -Sakahari
Type setting by: Maruti Business Systems
*P*rinted at:
Neo Imperial Printers, Chennai: 84

In Tamil:
100 மசாலா குருமா வகைகள்
100 பிரியாணி கலவை சாத வகைகள்
100 டிபன் வகைகள்
100 சுவையான சிற்றுண்டிகள்
100 மிக்ஸர், முறுக்குகள்
100 சூப்புகள், குளிர்பானங்கள்
100 சைவ மசாலா கறி வகைகள்
100 அருமையான புட்டிங்குகள்
100 ருசியான முட்டை சமையல்
100 நாளூறும் ஊறுகாய்கள்
100 தென்னிந்திய மைக்ரோ வேவ் சமையல்
100 புத்துணர்வு தரும் காய்,கனி, பானங்கள்
100 சட்னி வகைகள்
100 சோயா உணவுகள்
100 ருசியான முட்டை சமையல்
200 அறுசுவை மதிய உணவுகள்
200 இன்சுவை இனிப்புகள்
300 சர்க்கரை நோய்க்கேற்ற உணவுக் குறிப்புகள்
50 பொங்கல் பண்டிகை சமையல்
25 விநாயகர் சதுர்த்தி நைவேத்திய சமையல்
25 மக்காச்சோள உணவு வகைகள்
சுகமான சமையல் (சமையலறை ஆலோசனைகள்)

In Kannada:
100 Vegetabulu Gravigalu
100 Biriyani, fried rice bagaigal
100 Thindi bagaigalu
100 Upaharagalu
100 Ruchikaravaadha Shakahaara Palyagalu
100 Chakkuli Vaagu Mixturugalu
100 Dhakshina Bharathiya Microwave Adigagalu
200 Ruchikara Vootadha Thinusugalu
200 Sampradhayaka Sihi thnusugalu

PREFACE

This book "SNACKS SPECIAL" contains many specials such as Springrolls, Burgers, Pizzas, cutlets and also the regular South Indian traditional items such as Bondas, Bajjis, Pakodas etc. However many new variations (tastes) were induced into these items itself with simple changes so that they will be more cherished.

As you are aware there are some chutney varieties already given in my earlier book "100 TIFFIN VARIETIES". Some more chutney varieties used more with snacks are given at the end of this book. Tomato ketchup is more used with many snacks. The recipe for making TOMATO KETCHUP is also given at the end of this book.

The good response and appreciation of my earlier books has encouraged me to write this book. I thank one and all for the encouragement they have given me.

21.11.1991.

Mrs.S.Mallika Badrinath

INDEX

1. MINI VEGETABLE SAMOSA

Ingredients :

For the dough:
Maida - 2 cups
Oil - 4 Tbl. Sps.
Salt - ½ tsp.
Baking Powder - 2 pinches.
Ice cold water - for
mixing the dough
Oil - enough to deep fry.

For Masala:-
Onions - 2
Potatoes - ¼ kg.
Carrot - 2
Peas - 100 gms.
Beetroot - 1 small
French beans - 7
Salt - as required
Garam masala powder - ½ tsp.
Dry Mango powder - ½ tsp.
Green Chillies - 4
Cumin powder - ½ tsp.
Turmeric powder - ½ tsp.
Red chilli powder - ½ tsp.
Oil - for frying.

Method:-

DOUGH:-

1. Sieve maida twice with baking powder and salt.
2. Blend oil to flour with hands till it resembles fine bread crumbs.
3. Sprinkle cold water and knead to a stiff dough.
4. Knead well for several minutes till the dough becomes elastic and pliable.
5. Keep under wet cloth for ½ an hour.

MASALA:-

6. Cut onions lengthwise and other vegetables to small pieces.
7. Pressure cook potatoes. Peel and mash coarsely.
8. Steam other vegetables without adding water.
9. Mince green chillies.
10. Heat oil in a frying pan, add cumin seeds, minced chillies and then onion.
11. Fry till crisp. Add other vegetables and stir till moisture evaporates.
12. Add other powdered spices and remove from fire.

Preparation of Samosas:-

1. Divide the dough into 8 balls.
2. Roll out each ball into very thin chappathi using madia for dusting.
3. Apply 1 teaspoon of oil on one chappathi and dust little maida on top.
4. Keep second chappathi on top. Prepare in the same manner so that 4 chappathis are in one pile.
5. Roll lightly on top. Make rest of the dough in the same manner.
6. Heat a 'tawa' and place one pile of chappathis on top.
7. Gently turn over when it starts to bubble up.
8. After turning peel off the first layer.
9. Every time after turning over peel off top chappathi, so that all the chappathis are roasted on one side only.
10. Cut each chappathi into 2½ inch width strips like ribbon, keep covered under wet cloth each time.
11. Make a paste of maida by mixing it with just enough water (2 Tbl. sps. of maida).
12. Take one strip and make triangular pocket at one end, like a cone.
13. Seal the overlapping portion with maida paste (Shaded part shown in figure).

14. Keep little masala inside the pocket.
15. Fold and roll the strip in such a way that it remains in triangular shape. (Folding at each dotted lines as shown in figure).
16. At the end of overlapping seal with maida paste.
17. Prepare all the samosas and keep under a wet muslin cloth till the time of deep frying.
18. Deep fry few samosas at a time in hot oil (in reduced flame) till crisp and brown. Serve with tomato ketchup.

Note: For crisp samosas – The dough should be kneaded properly. Deep fry for a longer time in reduced flame.

Optional: The samosas can be deep fried till light brown colour (do not fry till full brown and and crisp) and keep them aside. Afterwards just before serving deep fry them again in reduced flame till crisp and brown.

Other Suggested Stuffings:

a. **Potato Samosa:** Make a masala with onions, potatoes and peas alone.

b. **Paneer Samosa:** Prepare masala with onions, sprouted green gram (steamed) and crumbled paneer with desired seasoning.

c. **Green Gram Samosa:** Steam sprouted green gram for 5 minutes. Grind coarsely. In oil fry chopped onions, tomatoes, ginger chilli paste and ground paste. Fry well and add garam masala, grated coconut and lime juice.

d. **Sweet Samosa:** Mix crumbled paneer with powdered sugar, grated fresh coconut, chopped nuts and raisins. (While making sweet samosas reduce salt in the dough).

e. **Khova Samosa:** Mix crumbled milk Khova with powdered sugar, tutti fruity pieces, almonds, kismis, cherries and dry grated coconut.

f. **Fruit Samosa:** Both khova and paneer can be mixed together with sugar, nuts and even tinned sliced pineapple pieces and cherries.

g. **Onion Samosa:** Mix Bengal gram flour with little oil, salt and just enough water to make stiff dough. Make thin chappathis and roast on a frying pan without oil till crisp. Cool and powder it. Sieve well. Fry lots of onions in oil. Add salt, chilli powder, sugar, garam masala powder, lime juice and powdered gram flour chappathis at the end. Use this as stuffing for Samosas.

h. **Green Peas Samosa:** Cook and grind peas to coarse paste. Heat little oil and fry crushed ginger, chopped onions and ground peas. Fry till moisture is absorbed. Add dhania powder, jeera powder, garam masala powder, salt, turmeric and red chilli powder. Mix well and remove from fire. Add grated fresh coconut, lime juice and coriander leaves. Use this as stuffing for Samosa.

2. KING SAMOSA

Ingredients:

For the dough:
Maida - 1 cup (heaped)
Baking Powder - ¼ tsp.
White butter - 60 gms. (2 heaped Tbl.Sps)
Salt - ½ tsp.
Ice cold water - to mix the dough.
Oil - enough to deep fry.

For Masala
Chopped onions - 1 cup
Potatoes - 4 (cooked)
Cooked Peas - ¼ cup
Aniseed - ½ tsp.
Dhania powder - 1 Tbl. sp.
'Am chur' - 1 tsp. (Dry Mango powder)
Black pepper powder - ½ tsp.
Ginger green chilli paste - 1½ tsp.
Salt - as required
'kala Namak' (black Salt) - ½ tsp.
Turmeric powder - ¼ tsp.
Garam masala powder - ½ tsp.

Method:
Dough:
1. Sieve maida twice with baking powder and salt.
2. Blend butter evenly with finger tips to the flour.
3. Sprinkle ice cold water and knead to a stiff dough.
4. Apply little oil to hands and knead the dough for nearly 10 to 15 minutes.
5. Keep closed under a wet cloth for 30 minutes.

Masala:
1. Heat oil in a deep pan and add aniseed and little dhania (optional).
2. Stir in ginger chilli paste and then onions.
3. Fry till crisp and add sugar, dhania powder, garam masala powder.
4. Put peeled mashed potatoes and peas.
5. Fry till good small comes and then sprinkle salt, turmeric, pepper and at the end 'Kala namak' and 'Am chur'. Remove from fire.

Preparation:
1. Make small balls from the dough.
2. Roll it out into circles of medium thickness.
3. Cut into two in the centre.
4. Place little filling in the centre.
5. Apply little water around the edges.
6. Fold straight lined edges to the Centre to form a cone.
7. Seal over lapping edges with water.

8. Press down all the edges well.
9. Prepare all the samosas like this and keep under a wet cloth or in Refrigerator (gives best results) for ½ an hour.
10. Heat oil in a deep curved pan and fry few samosas at a time in medium flame till crisp and brown. (Approximately 10 to 12 minutes).
11. Serve with sweet chutney, mint chutney or Tomato ketchup. [Recipe given at the end of this book.]

To prevent dosa from sticking to the dosa pan smear little powdered salt and wipe well just before making dosa.

5

3. KACHORIES

Ingredients:

For the dough:

Maida - 2 cups
Oil - 6 Tbl.sps.
Salt - 1 tsp.
Oil - Enough to deep fry

For stuffing:

Green gram dhal - 12 Tbl.sps.
De husked black gram
dhal - 1/3 cup
Bengal gram flour - 2 Tbl.sps.
Turmeric powder - ¼ tsp.
Dhania powder - 1 tsp.
Asafoetida - a pinch
Aniseed - ½ tsp.
(Powdered coarsely)
Red chilli powder - 1 tsp.
Ginger, green chilli paste - 2 tsps.
Salt - as required
Sugar - 1 tsp.
Lemon - 1.
Oil - 3 Tbl.sps.

Method:

Dough:

1. Add Salt, oil to Maida and mix well with finger tips till it resembles bread crumbs.
2. Sprinkle water and knead to a stiff dough
3. Knead well for few minutes till dough becomes pliable.
4. Keep closed with a wet muslin cloth for half an hour.

Stuffing

1. Soak black gram dhal in water for 6 hours.
2. Soak green dhal separately for 2 hours.
3. In a broad frying pan add black gram dhal and enough water to cover it.
4. When it is half cooked add green gram dhal and cook covered in low flame till dhal becomes tender and moisture is absorbed completely.
5. Remove from fire and cool down.
6. In a separate pan heat oil, add powdered aniseed, ginger chilli paste, dhania powder, red chilli powder and then gram flour.
7. Stir for a minute and then add turmeric, salt, sugar and then cooked dhal.
8. Mash and stir well until the mixture becomes dry.
9. Squeeze lemon, add chopped coriander leaves and remove from fire.

To Make:

1. Make small balls from the dough.
2. Roll into thick circles. (like puris)
3. Keep little stuffing, in the centre, close and make like a ball. (If necessary stick with little water).
4. Gently press on top to make it little flat.
5. Heat oil and deep fry few kachories at a time in reduced flame until golden brown and crisp.
6. Serve with sweet chutney and coriander chutney.

Sweet Chutney: Refer Panipuri.

Coriander Chutney:

Chopped coriander
leaves - 1½ cups.
Ginger - 2 inch piece
Tamarind - small lemon sized
Green chillies - 5
Jaggery and salt - as per taste.

Method:

Grind all the ingredients to smooth paste.
Serve with Kachoires.

Variation:

Green gram dhal kachories:

Heat little oil, add mustard minced green chillies, red chilli powder and then soaked green gram dhal (dehusked). Pour just enough water and little turmeric powder. Close with a lid and cook till dhal becomes soft and moisture is absorbed. Add salt, sugar, chopped coriander leaves, juice of lemon, powdered cinnamon and clove. Mix well and use this stuffing for making kachories.

4. PANI PURI

Ingredients:

Fine rawa - ¾ cup
Maida - ½ cup
Black gram flour -2 tsp (level)
(Dehusked Urad)
Salt - ¼ tsp.
Baking powder - 2 pinches
Ice cold water (or) Soda water - to
mix the dough
Oil - Enough to deep fry.

Method:

1. Dry roast urad dhal till golden brown in colour. Pound into fine powder in a mixie.
2. Mix Maida, rawa, urad flour, salt and baking powder in a bowl.
3. Add water and knead to a stiff dough.
4. Keep closed under a wet cloth for 10 minutes.
5. Pat and knead again till the dough becomes smooth and elastic.
6. Divide the dough into 4 parts and roll out each into big chappathi of medium thickness.
7. Using a round biscuit cutter, cut small rounds and deep fry in hot oil, till crisp and golden. (or) Make small even sized balls from the dough. Roll each into small circles and then deep fry.

Note: After rolling out keep them under wet cloth, before deep frying. Do not allow to dry out. Put one by one in hot oil and press well with laddle to puff up. Fry in medium flame till crisp and golden.

Greeen Chutney: (Pani)

Grind together:
Mint leaves - 1 cup
Chopped coriander leaves - ½ cup
Green chillies - 4
Cumin seeds - ½ tsp.
Powdered Kala Namak - 1tsp.
(Black salt)
Ordinary salt - as required.
Tamarind - Marble sized (soaked in water)

Method:

1. Grind the ingredients of green chutney to smooth paste with minimum water possible.
2. Strain and then keep aside for 3 to 4 hours.
3. Just before serving take the desired quantity and dilute with water as per taste. Lemon juice or dry mango powder can also be added if liked.
4. Grind sweet chutney to smooth paste. Strain through a tamarind strainer. Boil it for few minutes till it becomes thick sauce.

Sweet chutney:
(Grind together)
Tamarind - Lemon sized
(soak in water)
Grated jaggery - 5 tablespoons.
Seedless dates - 5
(Chopped and cooked in little water)
salt - 1 tsp.
Red chilli powder - ¼ tsp.

To Serve:

1. Soak green gram (whole) for 6 to 10 hours.
2. Pressure cook till one whistle.
3. Cook potatoes.
4. Peel and dice it.
5. Make a hole with thumb on top side of each puri.
6. Put little cooked gram and potato inside, with little sweet chutney and fill with pani. Serve immediately.

Note: Pani & Sweet chutney can be preserved in refrigerator for 3 days.

5. DAHI PURI

1. Prepare puris as mentioned in Pani puri
2. Whip fresh thick curds with little sugar and salt till creamy.
3. Fry cooked diced potatoes in oil with jeera, turmeric, salt, chilli powder and garam masala
4. Break each puri on top, keep little boiled potato pieces, cooked green gram (or) peas (or) channa.
5. Put one tsp of sweet chutney inside.
6. Fill in whipped curds.
7. Sprinkle sev, red chilli powder, salt, roasted jeera powder, little powdered kala Namak on top. Serve immediately.

> **Dry roast powdered salt before putting them in shakers for easy flow.**

6. BHEL PURI

Ingredients:

Crushed puri pieces from
previous recipe - 1 cup.

Crushed potato chips - ½ cup.

Puffed rice - 2 cups.
(pori)

Grated carrots - 2 Tbl.sps.

Finely cut onions - 1½ Tbl.sp.

Grated mango and cucumber - 1½
Tbl.sp.

Chopped coriander leaves - 1 Tbl.sp.

Finely cut tomatoes - 1 Tbl.sp.

*Sev - ½ cup.

Powedered salt- ½ tsp.

Red chilli powder - 1 tsp.

Cooked peas (or) Green gram with
cooked diced potatoes - 1½ Tbl.sps.

Sweet chutney - 3 tsps.

Mint chutney - 3 tsps.

Garlic chutney - 2 tsps.

Dry mango powder - ¼ tsp.

Garlic chutney:(Grind together)

Garlic - 15 flakes, Tamarind - little

Cumin seed - ½ tsp.

Red chilli powder - 1 tsp.

Salt - 1 tsp.

Method:

1. In a broad bowl mix crushed puris, chips, puffed rice and half of the sev.
2. Add prepared vegetables, dry powders and at the end all the chutneys.
3. Mix briskly, with laddle and serve immediately garnished with rest of the sev, cut onions and coriander leaves.

* Sev: This is savoury prepared from bengal gram flour. Mix bengal gram flour with salt and water and make a stiff dough. Using a sev press, squeeze directly on hot oil. Deep fry till crisp.

7. VEGETABLE FINGERS

Ingredients:

Green gram dhal - ½ cup
(Dehusked)

Ginger; Garlic paste -1 tsp.

Minced green chillies -1 tsp.

Finely cut onions - 3 Tbl.Sps.

Finely diced vegetables - ½ cup.

(Carrot, beans, cabbage, cauliflower etc).

Salt - as required.

Thick curds - 3 Tbl.sps.
(sour)

Cooking Soda - ¼ tsp.

Oil - To deep fry.

Method:

1. Soak dhal in water for 2 hours.
2. Grind to smooth paste without adding water. Add salt.
3. Steam diced vegetables in Pressure cooker for 3 minutes.
4. Heat little oil and fry ginger garlic paste, onions and then vegetables.
5. Add this to ground dhal with curds and soda.
6. Mix well and pour on greasd cooker plate and steam like Idlis.
7. Cool down and cut into fingers.
8. Deep fry in hot oil till crisp and serve hot.

8. MOONG FINGERS

Ingredients:

Green gram dhal - ½ cup
(Dehusked)
Bread - 8 slices
Finely cut Onions - 2 Tbl. Sps.
Salt - as required.
Chopped Coriander
leaves - 1 Tbl. Sp.
Red Chilli powder - ½ tsp.
Garam masala powder - ½ tsp.
Ginger, green chilli paste - 1½ tsp.
Oil - To deep fry.

Method:-

1. Cook dhal in enough boiling water till it splits.
2. Drain water completely and squeeze dhal to remove excess moisture. (Dhal water can be used for rasam or soup)
3. Dip bread slices one by one in water quickly and squeeze out moisture.
4. Add to the dhal with other ingredients.
5. Mix well and make lemon sized balls.
6. Shape into fingers and deep fry in hot oil till crisp.

Note:-

If the fingers losses its shape while frying (which shows that there is excess moisture) add little rice flour (or) dry bread crumbs, mix well and then shape it.

9. POTATO ROLLS

Ingredients:-

For the dough:-

Maida - 1 cup (heaped,
Fine rawa - ½ cup
Oil - 4 tsps.
Salt - ½ tsp.

For the Masala:-

Potatoes - ½ kg.
Finely cut onions - 3 Tbl. sps.
Chopped Coriander leaves - 2 tsps.
Ginger, green chilli paste - 1½ to 2 tsps.
Dry mango powder - 1 tsp. (Am-chur)
Tumeric powder - ½ tsp.
Red chilli powder - ½ tsp.
Garam masala powder - ¾ tsp.
Salt - as required.
Oil - for frying.

Make into paste:-

Maida - 2 Tbl. sps.
Water - 3 Tbl. sps.

Method:-

1. Mix maida, rawa, oil and salt together in a basin.
2. Using enough water knead to a smooth dough. (like chappathi dough). Keep closed.
3. Pressure cook potatoes with skin in enough water.
4. Peel and mash coarsely.
5. Add other raw ingredients and mix well.
6. Make medium sized balls from the prepared dough.
7. Rollout into medium sized chappathis.
8. Place filling lengthwise (handfull) on that chappathi at one corner leaving little gap behind.
9. Gently roll from that corner to other end.
10. Seal with maida paste at that end and sides of the roll.
11. Make all the rolls in the same manner and deep fry till crisp and golden brown.
12. While serving cut the rolls into three or four pieces.
13. Serve hot with tomato ketchup or sweet chutney.

10.   BREAD ROLLS

Ingredients Required:

Bread - 1 loaf.
Oil - for Deep frying.

For Masala:-

Boiled potatoes - ¼ kg.
Cooked peas - ½ cup.
Finely chopped cooked
vegetables - 1½ cup
(Carrots, beans cauliflower etc.)
Chopped onions - ½ cup.
Chopped capsicums - ¼ cup.
Ginger, greenchilli paste - 1½ tsps.
Red chilli powder - 1 tsp.
Garam masala powder - ½ tsp.
Turmeric powder - ¼ tsp.
Chopped coriander
leaves - 1Tbl. Sp.
Lemon - 1
Salt - as required.

Method:-

1. Heat oil in a deep curved pan and fry ginger chilli paste onions, capsicums till crisp.
2. Add other cooked vegetables, mashed potatoes and fry till moisture is absorbed.
3. Add turmeric, salt, chilli powder and garam masala.
4. Squeeze lime, garnish with coriander leaves and remove from fire.
5. Trim outer crusts from Bread slices.
6. Take a slice and dip it quickly in water and press inbetween palms to remove excess water (by keeping flat).
7. Keep a tablespoon of filling inside.
8. Close with wet hands and seal well to make oblong roll.
9. Make all the rolls, arrange in a plate and keep in refrigerator for 2 hours.
10. Deep fry in hot oil few rolls at a time till crisp and brown. Serve hot with tomato ketchup.

Variations:-

(1). Any left over dry curry (or) porial can be converted into delicious evening snack by using that as a filling for the rolls.
(2). Instead of making into rolls use two slices of bread which is dipped in water quickly. Keep filling inbetween both and seal by pressing flat. Sprinkle little rawa on both sides and press lightly with rolling bin. Deep fry in hot oil.

11. PANEER ROLLS

Ingredients:

*Paneer - From 1 litre milk
Onions - 2
Capsicums - 2 (small)
Salt - as required.
Bread slices - 6
Garam masala powder - ¼ tsp.
Minced green chillies - 1 tsp.
Red chilli powder - ½ tsp.
Maida - 2 tsps.
Corn flour - 2 tsps.
Fine rawa - 1 Tbl. sp.
Dhania powder - 1 tsp.
Chopped mint and coriander
leaves - 2 Tbl.sps.
Oil - To deep fry.

Method:-

1. Chop onions and capsicums into fine pieces.
2. Fry both in little oil till raw smell goes.
3. Crumble paneer well without any lumps.
4. Add maida, corn flour and knead like a dough.
5. Mix fried vegetables, chopped chillies, salt, red chilli. powder, garam masala, dhania powder and coriander leaves.
6. Dip bread slices one by one water quickly, squeeze out extra moisture and add to the dough.
7. Mix well, make balls and then shape it like fingers and roll on rawa.
8. Chill for ½ an hour.
9. Deep fry in hot oil till crisp. Serve hot with tomato ketchup.

* To make paneer - Boil milk. Reduce flame. Squeeze lime juice or add 1 cup of curds. Stir till milk curdles, strain through muslin cloth and hang for one hour. Use this paneer (cottage cheese) as in the recipe given.

Note:-
These rolls can also be made without adding bread.

12.   CARROT RISSOLES

Ingredients:

Cooked Rice - 1 cup.
(any left over rice is enough)
Carrots - 200 gms.
Onion - 1 large
Capsicum - 1 or 2
Salt - as required.
Red chilli powder - 1 tsp.
Garam Masala Powder - ½ tsp.
Fine bread crumbs - ¼ cup.
Corn flour - 1 Tbl. sp.
Rice flour - 3 Tbl. sps.
Oil - enough to deep fry.

Make into paste

Maida - 2 Tbl. sps.
Corn flour - 1 Tbl. sp.
Water - 6 Tbl. sps.

Method:-

1. Steam whole carrots and mash it to fine paste.
2. Chop onions and capsicum finely.
3. Heat little oil and fry onions, capsicum for few minutes.
4. Remove from fire and mix with mashed cooked rice, mashed carrots, half of the bread crumbs and other dry ingredients.
5. Make small balls.
6. Dredge on bread crumbs.
7. Then dip in maida paste and then roll on bread crumbs (Twice).
8. Arrange in a plate and keep in refrigerator for 1 hour.
9. Deep fry in hot oil till crisp.
10. Serve with ketchup.

Note:-
While mashing rice do not put in mixie. Mash well with a laddle or with hands.
While deep frying do not distrub in between. When golden brown underneath just turn once for even frying.

Variations:-
(1). Shape the balls into oblong rolls and then deep fry.
(2). Make like cutlets and shallow fry on a hot tawa.

13. DOUBLE BEAN RISSOLES

Ingredients:

Dry double bean seeds - 1 cup.
(broad, white variety)
Finely chopped spring
onions and onion
stem - ½ cup.
Salt - as required.
Finely chopped, coriander
leaves - 1½ Tbl. sps.
Coriander, cumin powder
(Dhania, Jeera) - ¼ tsp.
Oil - Enough to deep fry.

Grind to paste:-

Green chillies - 6
Garlic - 1 flake
Salt - a pinch.

Method:-

1. Soak bean seeds for one day. (20 to 24 hrs) in enough water.
2. Strain and remove the outer skin.
3. Grind to smooth paste without adding water. Add salt.
4. Mix with other ingredients.
5. Make balls using wet hands.
6. Deep fry in hot oil as balls (or) shape into fingers and fry till crisp and brown.
7. Serve hot with tomato ketchup.

18

14. CABBAGE STEAKS

Ingredients:

Bengal gram dhal - 1 cup.

Red chillies - 7

Poppy seeds - 2 tsps.

Cumin seeds - 1 tsp.

Cinnamon - 1 inch piece.

Garlic - 2 flakes.

Grated cabbage - 1½ cup.

Salt - as required.

Oil - for deep frying.

Method:-

1. Soak dhal in water for 2 hours.
2. Grind chillies, garlic and poppy to fine paste.
3. Add soaked dhal, salt and grind to coarse paste. (Do not add water while grinding).
4. Mix grated Cabbage to this and make oblong rolls. (1½ inch diameter and 6 to 8 inches length).
5. Arrange on a greased cooker plate.
6. Steam in pressure cooker for 5 to 7 mintes.
7. Cool down and cut into ½ inch thick discs. (round pieces).
8. Deep fry in hot oil till golden brown. Serve hot.

15. PESALU KADIYALU

Ingredients:

Green gram dhal - 3 Cups
Urad dhal - ½ Cups
Ripe Banana - 1
Rice flour - ¾ Cup
 (washed & dried)
Salt - 1 ½ tsp

To Serve with:

Coconut chutney
(or)
Tomato chutney
(or)
Any sweet payasam

Method:

1. Soak both kinds of dhal together in water.
2. Soak rice flour in little water for 10 minutes.
3. Drain water completely from dhal and grind to smooth frothy paste in stone grinder without using water.
4. Add rice flour paste, mashed banana at the end and grind for another minute. Add salt and remove.
5. Heat oil in a shallow, small frying pan.
6. Take 1½ ladle full of dough in a sharp edged container.
7. Pour into the hot oil in circular motion so that it forms a ring. (Both the ends should meet together)
8. When it turns golden, flip over in the oil carefully using a long spoon (or stick).
9. Remove from oil and drain well to remove extra oil.
10.Serve hot with mentioned side dishes as per taste.

16. RICE FLOUR RINGS

Ingredients:

*Rice Flour - 2 cups (heaped)
Water - 3 cups.
Salt - 2 tsps.
Oil - To deep fry.
Grated fresh coconut - 1½ Tbl. sps.

Powder Coarsely:

Black pepper - ½ tsp.
Cumin seeds - ½ tsp.

*Rice Flour

Wash and soak rice in water for half an hour. Drain water completely spread over a cloth and allow to dry under shade. Mill or pound to fine powder. Sieve and dry again for 2 days under shade. Preserve in air tight Container.

Method:-

1. Heat water in heavy vessel (or) deep frying pan.
2. Add salt, a teaspoon of oil and grated coconut to the water.
3. When it starts boiling reduce flame completely and put the flour as a heap in the centre of the water.
4. Insert a laddle and close with a lid.
5. Allow to cook for 7 to 10 minutes in reduced flame.
6. Remove from fire and stir briskly with laddle.
7. When it becomes luke warm add cumin, pepper powder, and knead well like chappathi dough. (If necessary sprinkle little warm water).
8. Knead smoothly using enough oil to handle the dough.
9. Make lemon sized balls.
10. Roll it out into fingers on oiled working surface.
11. Join both ends to form a ring.
12. Make all the dough in the same manner.
13. Deep fry in hot oil till goldern brown and crisp.
14. Serve with coconut chutney (or) pickle.

17. VEGETABLE FRITTERS

Ingredients:

Big onions - 3

Carrots - 3 (medium sized)

Cabbage - 200 gms.

Capsicum - 2

Aji-no-moto - ½ tsp.

Soya sauce - 2 tsps.

Chilli sauce - 2 tsps.

Tomato sauce - 1 Tbl.sp.

Salt - as required.

Red chilli powder - ½ tsp.

Fine bread crumbs - 2 Tbl.sps.

Corn flour - 1 Tbl.sp.

Maida - 1 Tbl.sp.

Bengal gram flour - 2 Tbl.sps.

Oil - To deep fry.

Method:-

1. Slice onions and capsicums into thin rings.
2. Chop carrots and cabbage into thin match stick like pieces.
3. Place all the chopped vegetables in ice cold water for ½ an hour.
4. Remove and wipe well with a towel.
5. Spread on a broad plate, mix with salt, chilli powder, aji-no-moto and all the sauces.
6. Allow to marinate for 10 minutes.
7. Sprinkle all the flours, bread crumbs to this and mix well.
8. Put in oil till it holds by crumbling with fingertips.
9. Deep fry till crisp. Drain well to remove excess oil. Serve hot.

18.   CAULIFLOWER FRITTERS

Ingredients:

Cauliflower -1 (large)
Turmeric powder - ¼ tsp.
Salt - as required.
Red chilli powder - ½ tsp.
Garam masala powder - ½ tsp.
Maida - ½ cup.
Rusk powder or
Fine bread crumbs - ½ cup.
Oil - enough to deep fry.

Method:-

1. Wash and separate cauliflower into medium sized flowerettes.
2. Heat water in a vessel to which Salt and turmeric powder is added.
3. When it starts boiling add Cauliflower pieces. Close with a lid and remove from fire.
4. After few minutes drain water completely. Dry well on a towel.
5. Sprinkle little salt, Chilli powder and garam masala powder to the pieces. Keep aside for 10 minutes.
6. Make a thick pase of Maida with water.
7. Dip cauliflower pieces in Maida paste and roll on bread crumbs.
8. Deep fry in hot oil till crisp. Serve hot with tomato ketchup.

Variations:

1. Half boiled cauliflower can be deep fried without dipping in maida paste.
2. Grind to smooth paste - cashewnuts, Poppy seeds, roasted gram, salt, aniseed, red chilli powder and garam masala powder, with minimum water possible. Mix with little maida, and rice flour. Dip boiled cauliflower in this and deep fry in hot oil.
3. Grind red chillies, dhania, Jeera, little soaked tamarind, coconut, turmeric powder, garam masala powder, littler raw rice (soaked in water) together with salt. Dip boiled cauliflower in this paste and deep fry.

19. CHINESE CAULIFLOWER MANCHURIAN (DRY)

Ingredients:

Cauliflower - 1 medium sized
Corn flour - 3 Tbl. sps. (heaped)
Salt - as required.
Soya sauce - 1 Tbl. sp.
Worcestershire sauce - 1Tbl. sp.
Aji-no-moto - ½ tsp.
Oil - for frying.

Grind together:

Ginger - 1 inch piece.
Garlic - 4 flakes.
Green chillies - 7.

Method:-

1. Separate flowerettes from Cauliflower.
2. Drop in boiling salted water for 2 minutes.
3. Drain off excess water.
4. Mix ground paste with salt, aji-no-moto and sauces.
5. Apply on cauliflower pieces and marinate for ½ an hour.
6. Sprinkle corn flour and deep fry in hot oil till brown.
7. Serve with sauce.

Variation:

Any other half cooked vegetable can be used to prepare manchurian like this.

20. POTATO FRITTERS

Ingredients:

Potatoes - ¼ kg.
Maida - 2 Tbl. sps.
Rice flour - 2 Tbl. sps.
Oil - enough to deep fry.

Grind together:

Aniseed - ¼ tsp.
Garlic - 6 flakes.
Ginger - 1 inch piece.
Red chillies - 8.
Roasted gram - 1½ Tbl. sp.
Salt - as required.

Variations:

Brinjal Fritters:

Slice medium sized tender brinjals, dip in the paste and then fry.

Method:

1. Select even sized potatoes.
2. Pressure cook with skin.
3. Peel and then slice into thin rounds.
4. Mix maida and rice flour to ground masala paste.
5. Apply this to potato slices and allow to marinate for ½ an hour.
6. Deep fry (or) shallow fry on a hot tawa with liberal oil till crisp and brown in reduced flame.

21. BANANA FRITTERS

Ingredients:

Raw banana - 2
(Plantain)
Oil - enough to deep fry.

Grind together:

Soaked bengal gram dhal - ½ cup.
Red chillies - 10
Dhania - 1½ tsps.
Small Onions - 3 or 4
(peeled)
Salt - ½ tsp.
Tamarind - little.

Method:

1. Scrape outer skin from Bananas and cut ½ inch thick round slices. Soak in salted water till required.
2. Soak dhal in water for one hour.
3. Drain water and grind with other ingredients to smooth paste.
4. Smear on both sides of bananas and arrange on a plate to marinate for ½ an hour.
5. Deep fry few pieces at a time in hot oil till crisp and golden. Serve hot.

22. BREAD FRITTERS

Ingredients:

Bread slices - 6
Bengal gram flour - ¼ cup.
Rice flour - 2 Tbl. Sps.
Salt - as required.
Red chilli powder - ¼ tsp.
Garam masala powder - ½ tsp.
Grated onion - 3 Tbl. sps.

Grind together:

Green chillies - 3
Coriander leaves - 1 Tbl.sp.
Salt - a pinch.
Ginder - small piece.

Method:

1. Cut each bread slice into 4 pieces.
2. Mix ground paste with onion, rice flour, bengal gram flour and other dry ingredients. Make into a paste with enough water. (Like Bajji batter).
3. Dip slices in the batter and shallow fry on a hot tawa with enough oil till brown.
4. Serve as an evening snack for children.

23. POTATO CHEESE CROQUETTES

Ingredients:

Potatoes - ¼ kg.
Grated Cheese - ½ cup.
Finely cut onions - ¼ cup.
Minced green chillies - 1 tsp.
Red chilli powder - ½ tsp.
Salt - as required.
Dry bread crumbs - ½ cup.
Corn flour - ¼ cup.
Oil - for frying.

Method:

1. Pressure cook potatoes. Peel and mash when it is still warm.
2. Mix grated cheese, onions, salt, chilli paste and red chilli powder with mashed potatoes.
3. Add half of the corn flour and bread crumbs to that.
4. Mix well and make small balls.
5. Flatten and make different shaped croquettes.
6. Make a paste of corn flour and water.
7. Dip the croquettes in it and dust with bread crumbs.
8. Deep fry in hot oil till crisp.
9. Serve with tomato ketch up.

Note: Shape the croquettes like triangle, diamond, spade shaped, heart shaped, rectangle, square and round. Makes a good snack for birthday parties. A tooth pick inserted on top with a small piece of cucumber (or) tomato makes it more attractive for the children to eat.

24. POTATO BASKETS

Ingredients:

Potatoes - ½ kg.
Corn flour - 2 Tbl.sps.
Salt - as required.
Any sundal or Vegetable filling.

Method:

1. Scrape outer skin and grate potatoes. (Do not put in water)
2. Press well in between two layers of a towel.
3. Sprinkle corn flour on top of it and spread a thin layer inside a small frying basket (or) small metal mesh strainers (with handle).
4. Press on top with another smaller frying basket which goes inside exactly.
5. Keep in hot oil till golden brown and crisp.
6. Sprinkle salt on top and serve with any filling.
7. Dot with sauce and serve.

Note: This can be made previously and preserved air tight containers for a week. For parties make a big basket for centre piece and other smaller ones around that to make it more attractive. Any salad or even sweet filling can be used. Do not sprikle salt if sweet filling is used.

25. VEGETABLE PUFFS

Ingredients:

For the pastry dough:

Maida - 225 gms (1½ alak)
Margarine
    or
Vanaspathi - 100 gms
(Approximately 3 heaped Tbl.sps.)
Salt - 1 tsp (level)
Ice cold water.

For the Masala:

Finely cut onions - 2 Tbl.sps.
Potatoes - 3 (or) 4 (Medium sized)
Turmeric powder - ¼ tsp.
Shelled peas - 2 Tbl.sps.
   (Fresh)
Salt - as required.
Carrot - 1
Beans - 5
Garam masala powder - ½ tsp.
Red chilli powder - ½ tsp.
Lemon - 1
Oil - for frying.

Method:

1. Sieve Maida with salt. Add ice cold water and knead to a stiff dough.
2. Pat and knead well for several times on a floured board till dough becomes elastic in nature.
3. Keep covered with a wet cloth for ½ an hour.

Masala:

1. Pressure cook whole potatoes (with skin) chopped carrots, beans and peas.
2. Peel skin from potatoes and mash coarsely.
3. Heat oil in a frying pan add cumin seeds and then ground masala paste.
4. Mix onions and stir till it becomes crisp.
5. Sprinkle garam masala powder, chilli powder, salt, turmeric and then add other cooked vegetables.
6. Fry well for few minutes. Squeeze lime, garnish with coriander and remove from fire.

To make puffs:

1. Knead the dough once again till it becomes elastic in nature.
2. Melt Vanaspathi and then keep a side for 10 to 15 minutes. When it hardens whip it well with a spoon, till creamy.
3. Divide it equally to 3 portions.

Make into paste:

Ginger - ½ inch piece.
Garlic - 3 flakes.
Green chillies - 2.

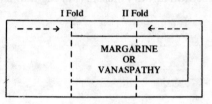

4. Take the complete kneaded dough on a working surface and roll it out into a large rectangle using maida for dusting.
   (rolled sheet should be as thin as possible.)
5. Apply one part of the Vanaspathi to 2/3 of the rectangle leaving ½ an inch all around as shown in figure below.
6. Fold the empty portion first and other side on top of it. Roll it lightly and repeat the same process twice more to use up all the Vanaspathi. (Refrigerate in between if you are not able to roll out properly to make the dough little firm).
7. Cut into small rectangles (3" x 4"). Keep little prepared stuffing inside and fold across. Seal edges with little water. Chill it for half an hour.
8. Pre heat the oven at 250°C. Brush the baking tray with water. Arrange puffs on that leaving enough gap in between.
9. Brush little milk (or egg whites) on top and bake till top layer turns golden brown. (Approximately 40 to 50 minutes) Serve hot.

Note: 1. Make a firm dough and then knead it well to make pliable. Otherwise dough will tear while rolling it into a thin sheet. Baking can be done in 50/50 sandwich maker (electrical) also instead of oven.
2. A mixture of soft butter and margarine can be used in the above receipe.
3. To make a triangle puff cut the pastry into squares, keep little filling inside andfold across diagonally. Seal with water.

26. VEGETABLE CONES

Prepare puff pastry as mentioned in previous receipe. Cut rolled out pastry into thin long strips. Apply little butter to small metal cones. Starting from the sharp end wrap the cones with strips gently over lapping on each round. Bake in moderate oven till it changes its colour. Brush with melted fat. When it cools down remove the metal cones. Stuff any dry masala (or) vegetable filling inside the cones and serve immediately.

Variation:

Deep fried cones:

Mix maida, little rawa, baking powder, salt and little butter together. Make a stiff dough with just enough water. Knead well. Roll out into thin oblong sheet and cut into strips. Wrap on cones as mentioned. Deep fry in hot oil with the metal cones. While frying cones separate in the oil itself. Remove carefully. Keep any desired stuffing.

27. VOL-AU-VENT CASES

This is an interesting variation made from Puff pastry. Prepare puff pastry as metnioned in vegetable puff. After folding and rolling process keep covered in refrigerator for ½ an hour. Roll lightly so that prepared pastry should be thicker than puffs. Take two round biscuit cutters with 4 inches diameter and 3 inches diameter. First cut circles using 4 inch cutter. Using the other cutter press down the circles gently half way through. Bake in a hot oven for 10 minutes. Using a sharp knief gently lift the centre portion which forms a cover to the cases. Bake again till done. Serve with any desired filling inside.

Note: Instead of using margarine or Vanaspathi alone mix soft butter with margarine or Vanaspathi and do the receipe.

28.   BAKED BRINJALS

Ingredients:

Big brinjals - 3
(Bajji variety)
Maida - ¼ cup.
Rice flour - 2 Tbl.sps.
Cooking cheese - 100 gms.
Tomato ketchup - ¼ cup.
Salt - as required.
Red chilli powder - ½ tsp.
Pepper powder - ¼ tsp.
Fine bread crumbs - ½ cup.
Oil - for deep frying.

Method:

1. Slice brinjals into thin circles.
2. Soak in salted water till required.
3. Mix maida, rice flour, salt, red chilli powder with just enough water to make a thick batter.
4. Wipe brinjals with a towel, dip in maida paste to coat on both sides and dredge on bread crumbs.
5. Deep fry in hot oil till crisp. Drain excess oil in a colander.
6. Grease a baking tray with butter or oil and arrange brinjals as a thin layer.
7. Sprinkle salt, pepper and spread little tomato ketchup on top and then sprinkle little grated cheese.
8. Repeat like this as layers till ¾th of the container. Top layer should be with grated cheese.
9. Bake in a preheated oven till cheese melts and changes in its colour lightly. Serve hot.

29.   STUFFED CAPSIUM

Ingredients:

Medium sized capsicums - 6

Chopped onions - ¼ cup

Finely cut steamed
vegetables - 2 cups.
(carrots, cauliflower, beans,
potatoes, peas, cabbage).

Roasted, powdered cumin
seeds - ¾ tsp.

Garam masala powder - ½ tsp.

Turmeric powder - ½ tsp.

Red chilli powder - ½ tsp.

Green chilli paste - 1 tsp.

lemon - 1

Bengal gram flour - 1½ Tbl.sps.

Salt - as required.

Oil - for frying.

Chopped coriander
leaves - 1 Tbl.sp.

Method:

1. Wash and cut capsicums horizontally into two.
2. Remove seeds and pith.
3. Immerse in boiling, salted water for 3 minutes.
4. Remove from water and drain well.

For filling:

5. Heat oil and fry onions till crisp.
6. Add red chilli powder, green chilli paste, masala powder and stir well.
7. Mix cooked drained vegetables, turmeric powder and fry till moisture is absorbed.
8. Add salt, cumin powder and mix well.
9. Squeeze lime and garnish with chopped coriander leaves.
10. Stuff the filling in capsicums.
11. Pat well and apply a thick paste of bengal gram flour on top.
12. Heat little oil in a flat frying pan and arrange capsicums in that.
13. Cover with a lid and cook in low flame.
14. Turn over carefully and fry till done on all sides.
15. If necessary add more oil while frying.
16. Serve hot sprinkled with tomato ketchup.

Variations:

1. This can be baked in an oven. (190°C for nearly 30 to 40 minutes approximately) while baking seal top with bread (which is soaked in water, squeezed and made into a thick paste) or Sprinkle grated cheese and bake till top layer turns brown.

2. Instead of vegetables use cooked corn for stuffing.

3. Boiled potatoes and peas alone can be used to prepare stuffing.

4. Chop 'Paneer' into small pieces (or) Crumble it well. Add fried onions, chillies, spring onions with salt and masala powder. Use as a stuffing inside capsicums.

5. Instead of cutting the capsicums into two, carefully cut top portion like a cap and do the receipe.

30. STUFFED TOMATOES

Ingredients:

Even sized firm ripe tomatoes - 8

Chopped onions - ¼ cup.

Finely chopped spring
    onion stem - ¼ cup.

Cooked peas - ½ cup.

Cooked carrots and
    cauliflower - ½ cup.

Worcestershire sauce - 2 tsps.

Salt - as required.

Pepper powder - ½ tsp.

Red chilli powder - ½ tsp.

Grated cheese - 2 Tbl.sps.

Oil - for frying.

Chilli sauce or capsico
    sauce - 2 tsps.

Method:

1. Slice thin top from tomatoes.
2. Carefully remove the seeds and pith using a spoon or scooper.
3. Put it upside down on a plate to drain out moisture.
4. Heat little oil and fry onions till crisp.
5. Add scooped out pulp and fry till moisture evaporates.
6. Add other vegetables and fry well.
7. Stir in salt, pepper, red chilli powder, sauces and keep in low flame till moisture is absorbed completely.
8. Fill in the tomatoes and sprinkle grated cheese on top.
9. Arrange on a greased oven proof dish.
10. Bake in a pre heated oven at 180°C for half an hour.
11. Serve garnished with finely cut coriander leaves.

Note: Tomatoes should be chilled before slicing. Keep in refrigerator (or) ice cold water to make it firm.

31. PIZZA

Ingredients:

For PIZZA NAN:

Maida - 2 cups (heaped)

Oil - 4 tsps.

Salt - ½ tsp.

Fresh yeast - 1 tsp.

(OR)

Dry yeast - ¾ tsp.

Milk - ½ cup.

Luke warm water - to mix the dough.

For TOPPING

Onions - 2

capsicums - 2

Tomatoes - 2

Cooking cheese - 50 gms.

Tomato sauce - 3 Tbl.sps.

Salt and pepper - as required

Butter - 1 Tbl.sp.

Method:

1. Soak yeast in luke warm milk for 10 to 15 minutes with little sugar.
2. Mix maida, salt and oil together in a bowl till it blends well.
3. Make a dent in the centre and pour milk, yeast mixture.
4. Gather flour with finger tips, add more warm water and mix to a soft dough. (Like chappthi dough consistency).
5. Do not knead it.
6. Keep covered in a warm place for 5 to 6 hours till it doubles in its volume.
7. Divide the dough into two parts equally.
8. Roll it out gently using maida like a thick chappathi.
9. Prick on top with fork in many places.
   (This helps the dough not to puff up while baking)
10. Pre heat oven at 275°C.
11. Arrange Nan on a greased oven proof dish an bake for 5 to 7 minutes.
12. Remove from oven and apply little butter on top.
13. Spread sauce evenly leaving 1 inch gap all around.
14. Arrange thinly sliced onions, capsicums and tomatoes (circles) on top of that.
15. Sprinkle with salt, pepper, and then grated cheese.
16. Bake again till cheese melts. Serve hot.

Variations:

1. Instead of tomato sauce use a mixture of worcestershire sauce, chilli sauce and tomato sauce.
2. In little oil fry aniseeds, chopped onions and tomatoes. Sprinkle salt, chilli powder, garam masala. Use as a topping on top of pizza with grated cheese and then bake.
3. Soak Rajma (red kidney beans) for 8 to 10 hours. Pressure cook for 20 minutes. Drain water completely, Fry onions, Add garam masala powder, dhania powder salt and red chilli powder. Add tomato sauce, mix well with beans. Use as topping for pizza.
4. Cook chopped palak (spinach) in just enough water. Grind Well and add salt, pepper, chilli powder, masala powder and tomato sauce. Apply on top of half baked pizza. Put one more layer of crumbled paneer. Arrange thinly cut spring onons and grated cheese on top. Bake till cheese melts.
5. Stir fry thinly sliced onions, spring onions, capsicums, carrots and cabbage with Aji-no-moto. Add salt, pepper, soya sauce and any other sauce. Use as topping.
6. Apply little butter on both sides of the half baked pizza. Fry on a hot tawa pressing both sides well. Serve with any vegetables gravy.

Note: Half baked pizzas stays good for few days if kept in plastic overs in refrigerator. (These pizza nan's are available in leading departmental stores also). Use cooking cheese which melts easily while baking. After spreading the toppings on half baked pizzas, it can be grilled.

38

32. MOONG DHAL BANZI

Ingredients:

Green gram(whole) - 1 cup (heaped)
Cooked potatoes - 3 or 4
Cooked peas - ¾ cup.
Green chillies - 15
Ginger - ½ inch piece
Asafoetida - 2 pinches.
Sugar - ½ tsp.
Cooking soda - ½ tsp.
Salt - as required.
Finely cut coriander
    leaves - 2½ Tbl.sps.
Chopped onions - ½ cup.
Oil - for frying.

Method:

1. Soak green gram for 8 hours.
2. Grind coarsely with ginger, green chillies and salt (without adding water).
3. Peel and mash potatoes well.
4. Crush peas coarsely.
5. To the ground paste add fried onions, potatoes, peas chopped coriander leaves, sugar, soda and a table spoon of oil. (It should be like a thick dough).
6. Take two plantain leaves and grease little oil on both sides.
7. Pat a handfull of mixture on top of a leaf and cover with another leaf.
8. Heat a 'tawa' and put it on top.
9. When the leaf turns black, turn over and cook. (Fry in low flame for longer time).
10. Take out the leaf and serve with onion chutney or coconut chutney.

Note: If plantain leaf is not available pat directly on top of 'tawa'. Cook in reduced flame, with enough oil.

33. HANDVO

Ingredients:

Bengal gram flour - 1 cup.
Rice flour - 1 cup.
Salt - 1½ tsp.
chopped coriander leaves - ½ cup.
seasame seeds - ¾ tsp.
Roasted gram - 1 Tbl.sp.
Coriander seeds - ½ tsp.
Sour butter milk - 2 cups.
Asafoetida - 2 pinches.
Cooking soda - ¼ tsp.

For seasoning:

Oil - 1 Tbl.sp.
Mustard - ½ tsp.
Curry leaves - 1 Tbl.sp.

Grind together:

Green chillies - 10
Ginger - 1 inch piece.
Garlic - 1 flake.

Method:

1. Mix gram flour and rice flour together with roasted gram, seasame seeds, coriander seeds, salt and soak in butter milk.
2. Keep aside for 8 to 10 hours. (to ferment)
3. Just before cooking add soda, ground paste, chopped coriander and asafoetida.
4. Heat oil, add seasonings and pour over handvo mix.
5. Stir gently to blend ingredients together.
6. Heat a small 'Kadai' (deep frying pan) with 1½ Tbl.Sp. of oil.
7. Pour ¼th of the handvo mix.
8. Close with a lid and cook in reduced flame till upper surface becomes dry.
9. Gently turn over and add more oil.
10. Close the lid and cook in reduced flame till both the sides are golden red in colour. (Approximately 10 to 15 minutes).
11. Cut into pieces before serving.

Note: If a broad kadai is used complete dough can be cooked at one time.

This can be baked in oven also.

40

34. KHANDVI

Ingredients:

Bengal gram flour - 1 cup.
Butter Milk - 2½ cups.
(little sour)
Salt - as required.

Grind together:

Ginger - 1 inch piece.
Green chillies - 8 to 10.
Asafoetida - a pinch.
Turmeric powder - a pinch.

For Seasoning:

Oil - 3 Tbl.sps.
Mustard - ½ tsp.

For garnishing:

Grated fresh coconut - 2 Tbl.sps.
Finely chopped coriander
    leaves - 2 Tbl.sps.

Method:

1. Mix gram flour, butter milk, Salt and ground paste without forming lumps, in a vessel.
2. Pressure cook in reduced flame for 20 to 30 minutes.
3. Remove from fire and cool down.
4. Place a heavy bottom kadai on stove and put khandvi mixture in it. (Do not add oil).
5. Stir in reduced flame. (Approximately 7 to 10 minutes)
6. To test the dough, put little dough on a greased flat plate.
7. Spread thinly. Try to roll it.
8. If it rolls without breaking khandvi is ready.
9. Pour the dough on a greased plate and pat with wet hands to thin layer. (back side of plate should be used)
10. Cut into thin strips.
11. Roll each strip from one end to the other like a swiss roll.
12. Arrange on a plate.
13. Heat little oil, add mustard and when it splutters pour over the strips.
14. Garnish with grated coconut and chopped coriander leaves.

Note: Rolling should be done immediately after patting on plate. (when it is still warm). If it cools down, rolling becomes impossible.

35. SPRING ROLLS

Ingredients:

For Dough:

Maida - 2 cups (heaped)
Oil - 4 Tbl.sps.
Baking powder - 2 pinches
Cooking Soda - 2 pinches.
Salt - 1 tsp.
Water - enough to mix
Little maida - for dusting.

Make into paste: (1)

Oil - 4 tsps.
Maida - 2½ tsps.

Make into paste: (2)

Water - 2 Tbl.sps.
Maida - 3 tsps.

For Masala:

Finely shredded Cabbage - 2 cups.
Grated Carrots - 1½ cup.
Chopped Cauliflower - 1 cup.
Finely chopped Capsicum 1 cup.
Chopped spring Onions - ¾ cup.
Chopped spring onion
        stalks - ½ tsp.

Method:

For the Dough

1. Sieve maida twice with soda, baking powder and salt.
2. Blend oil to the flour evenly using finger tips.
3. Sprinkle water and knead to a stiff dough.
4. Using a greased working surface knead well for several minutes till the dough becomes pliable.
5. Keep closed with a wet cloth for ½ an hour.

Masala:

1. Heat 4 Table spoons of oil in a broad frying pan.
2. Add ground paste and then onion.
3. Fry for a minute and then add Capsicum, carrot, Cabbage and at the end spring onion stem.
4. Stir fry in high flame for few minutes.
5. Add Aji - no - motto and then salt.
6. Fry till vegetables are done.
7. Sprinkle all the sauces and cook till dry. Remove from fire.

Preparation of Rolls:

1. For one roll make 2 small balls from the dough.
2. Roll each ball separately into puri sized circles.
3. Seal both the puris with little paste No. 1.
4. Using maida for dusting roll into thin, oblong chappathi.
5. Spread 2 Table spoons of masala little above one corner.

42

"Aji - no - motto" - ½ tsp.
Soya sauce - 1½ csp.
Chilli sauce - 1 tsp.
Tomato sauce - 1 tsp.
Worcestershire sauce - 1 tsp.
Salt - as required.
Sugar - ½ tsp.
White pepper powder - ½ tsp.
Oil - for frying.

<u>Grind to paste:</u>

Garlic - 3 flakes.
Red Chilli powder - ¾ tsp.

6. Apply paste No. 2 to complete edges of the chappathi.
7. First close the sides and then roll from one end (where the filling is kept) to the other end to form a cylinder.
8. Make all the rolls in the same manner.
9. Grease a cooker plate with oil and arrange few rolls leaving enough gap in between.
10. Steam in pressure cooker (like that of idlis) for 2 minutes.
11. Deep fry in hot oil till crisp and golden. (in medium flame).
12. Serve hot with tomato sauce or chilli sauce.
13. Cut each roll into 4 or 5 pieces before serving.

* Aji - no - motto — This is also called as chinese salt. Chemical name is Monosodium glutamate. Available in all leading departmental stores.

<u>Note:</u> If the dough is not kneaded properly rolls split in the centre while steaming.
For parties these rolls can be made previous day. After steaming keep it in plastic covers with enough space in between. Seal well. Keep in freezer compartment in Refrigerator. Take out half an hour before deep frying.

36. WONTONS

Ingredients:

For the Dough:

Maida - 1 cup (heaped)
Corn flour - ¼ cup.
Baking powder - ¼ tsp.
Oil - 2 tsp.
Salt - ½ tsp.
Ice cold water - to mix the dough.

Masala:

Prepare as mentioned in
previous receipe.

Method:

1. Sieve maida, corn flour, baking powder and salt together.
2. Add oil and blend well.
3. Knead to a stiff dough with ice cold water. (Refer previous recipe for mixing the dough)
4. Divide the dough into two portions and roll out each into thin rectangle.
5. Cut into 4 inch square pieces.
6. Keep little vegetable filling inside and smear edges with corn flour paste.
7. Lift all the four corners up and bring to the centre.
8. Over lap and seal with corn flour paste. (To form an envelope)
9. Keep under wet cloth till all the dough is used up.
10. Deep fry in hot oil in medium flame till crisp and brown. Serve hot with sauce.

Variations:

Different interesting shapes can be prepared with the dough. Make a round and bring the corners together up to form a 'money bag' shape. Cut into rectangles and fold like purse. Make one medium sized round and another small round. Keep filling on top of big round. Keep small one on top. Smear edges withcorn flour paste and shape like a cap. Cut the rolled sheet into squares. Keep little (½ tsp.) stuffing little below centre. Fold from below to cover it. Turn it to next side. Fold again. Bring the folded edges together to its centre. seal with little water. This also forms a cap.

37. CRISPY TOASTS

Ingredients:

Bread - 1 loaf.
Oil - For frying.
Boiled potatoes - ½ kg.
Vinegar - 2 Tbl. sps.
Prepared chinese masala as in
spring rolls.
Maida paste.
Fine bread crumbs.

Method:-

1. Remove brown crusts from the bread slices.
2. Prepare masala as mentioned in spring rolls.
3. Peel outer skin from boiled potatoes and mash well when it is still warm.
4. Mix with vegetable masala, vinegar, with little more salt and pepper powder.
5. Press little masala on top of bread slices on one side only.
6. Mix maida with water to make a thin paste.
7. Apply little paste on the vegetable side of toasts.
8. Sprinkle bread crumbs and press well. (Keep in refrigerator for ½an hour)
9. Heat oil and deep fry few slices at a time by putting vegetable side down in oil.
10. Then turn over and fry till crisp and brown.
11. Drain on absorbant paper to remove excess oil.
12. Serve by cutting into squares or fingers with different types of sauces.

Note:

Do not use fresh bread as it consumes more oil. This can be shallow fried on a hot 'tawa' with just enough oil.

Variation:

1. Make a filling with sprouted green gram and spring onions alone. Mix with mashed potatoes and do the recipe.
2. Instead of bread crumbs use rawa or fine vermicelli bits (half cooked) on top of vegetable mixture.
3. Make masala with onions, tomatoes and boiled potatoes alone and do the recipe.

38.   VEGETABLE PAN CAKE

Ingredients:

For the dough:

Maida - 3 cups (heaped)

Powdered Salt - 1¼ tsp.

Water - enough to mix the dough

Oil - for roasting.

For the filling:

Finely chopped spring onion.
tops - ½ cup.

Grated carrot - ¼ cup.

Grated Cabbage - ¼ cup.

Finely chopped white
onions - ¼ cup.

Thinly sliced green
chillies - 1½ tsp.

Mix everything together with
enough salt.

Method:-

1. Mix salt and water to maida and make a stiff dough.
2. Knead well for 5 to 10 minutes till the dough becomes pliable. (Do not add oil or any other fat).
3. Keep closed under a wet cloth for ½ an hour.
4. Divide the dough into 12 balls.
5. Roll out each into thin rectangle using maida for dusting.
6. Brush oil on top evenly.
7. Sprinkle little prepared vegetable filling on top evenly.
8. Roll from one end to other to form a cylinder.
9. Wind like a coil and make ball again.
10. Roll out into a thick chappathi.
11. Fry on a hot 'tawa' with just enough oil to roast on both sides till golden brown. Serve hot.

39. MIXED VEGETABLE KABAB

Ingredients:

Onions - 2
Carrots - 3
French beans - 100 gms.
Potatoes - ¼ kg.
Raw banana - 1
Beetroot - 1 small.
Chopped coriander
leaves - 2 Tbl. sps.
Oil - Enough to deep fry.
Bengal gram flour - 3 Tbl. sps.
Dry bread crumbs - 3 Tbl. sps.
Fresh bread - 6 slices.
Fresh cream - 1 Tbl. Sp.
Salt - as required.

Grind to paste:

Garlic - 4 flakes
Ginger - ½ inch piece.
Poppy seeds - 1 tsp.
Green chillies - 4.
Red chilli powder - ¾ tsp.
Cumin seed - ½ tsp.
Ani seed - ¼ tsp.
Cardamoms - 2
Black pepper - ½ tsp.
Vinegar - 2 tsps.
Cinnamon - small piece.
Cloves - 2.

Method:-

1. Pressure cook potatoes, Peel and mash well.
2. Grate onions. Steam whole carrots, Peeled beetroot and chopped beans.
3. Steam raw banana with skin in cooker for 5 minutes (under pressure). Peel and mash well.
4. Grate cooked carrots and beetroot.
5. Heat little oil and fry grated onion till golden brown.
6. Add masala paste with salt and sugar.
7. Stir constantly till raw flavour is lost.
8. Add prepared vegetables and fry till moisture evaporates.
9. Remove from fire and mix bengal gram flour, bread crumbs and soaked, squeezed bread slices.
10. Knead well and make even sized balls.
11. Then shape into thin cylinder and deep fry in hot oil till crisp and brown.
12. Serve hot with mint Chutney, tomato ketchup, sweet chutney and sliced, raw onions which is sprinkled with salt, pepper and lemon juice.

Note:

Insert Kabab in knitting needle and fry in deep hot oil turning all the sides well. (or) Apply on greased skewers and bake in oven till brown. Apply little butter when it is still hot and serve.

40. POTATO KABABS

Ingredients:

Potato - ¼ kg.
Bread - 7 slices.
Minced green chillies - 1½ tsp.
Chopped Coriander and mint
leaves - 2 Tbl. sps.
Garam masala powder - ½ tsp.
Dhania powder - 1 tsp.
Turmeric powder - ¼ tsp.
Rice flour - 3 Tbl. sps.
'Am chur' - ½ tsp.
(Dry mango powder)
Salt - as required.
Oil - enough to fry.

Method:-

1. Pressure cook potatoes. Peel and mash thoroughly when it is still warm.
2. Soak bread slices one by one in water and lift out immediately.
3. Squeeze extra moisture and add to mashed potatoes with all other dry ingredients.
4. Make balls and shape into Kababs.
5. Deep fry in hot oil till crisp and brown.
6. Serve hot with sauce or chutney.

41. BOTTLE GOURD KABABS

Ingredients:

Grated bootle gourd - 2 cups.
(heaped)

Bengal gram dhal - ¾ cup.

Ginger (cut into strips) - 1 tsp.

Finely cut onions - 2 Tbl. Sps.

Chopped coriander - 1 Tbl. Sp.
  leaves.

Salt - as required.

Garam masala powder - ½ tsp.

Oil - To deep fry.

Grind to paste:

Garlic - 2 flakes.

Ginger - ¼ inch piece.

Green chillies - 7.

Method:-

1. Wash dhal and take in a vessel with grated gourd and ginger strips.
2. Place the vessel in pressure cooker and cook till one sound.
3. To dry up excess moisture after cooking dry roast this in a pan for few minutes (without oil).
4. Grind coarsely and then mix salt, Coriander leaves, garam masala, Onions and ground paste.
5. Make lemon sized balls and shape like fingers.
6. Deep fry in hot oil till crisp.

42. MINTY KABABS

Ingredients:

Potatoes - ½ kg.

Sprouted green gram - ½ cup

Finely cut onions - ¼ cup.

Carrots - 3.

Bread slices - 8.

Dry bread crumbs

(Or)

Rusk powder - 3 Tbl. Sps.

Salt - as required.

Bengal gram flour - 5 Tbl. sps.

Garam masala powder - ½ tsp.

Oil - To deep fry.

Grind together with minimum water possible:

Green chillies - 6

Red chillies - 4

Garlic - 3 flakes

Ginger - 1 inch piece.

Mint leaves - ¼ cup.

Roasted gram - 1 Tbl. sp.

Method:-

1. Pressure cook whole potatoes and carrots.
2. Peel and mash well.
3. Steam sprouted green gram in cooker for 3 minutes.
4. Heat oil and fry onions till crisp.
5. Add cooked gram and fry till moisture gets absorbed.
6. Stir in ground paste and fry till raw smell goes.
7. Sprinkle bengal gram flour and stir for 2 minutes in reduced flame.
8. Add mashed potatoes, carrots with salt, garam masala and fry for few minutes.
9. Remove from fire and cool down.
10. Add bread slices which is dipped in water and squeezed well.
11. Mix in bread crumbs and shape into kababs.
12. Bake in oven with skewers, or deep fry in hot oil.

Note:

Do not disturb while deep frying. Turn once when it is done. If Kabab looses its shape while frying add some corn flour or bread crumbs to the vegetable mixture.

43. CAULIFLOWER KABABS

Ingredients:

Bengal gram dhal - 1 cup.

Cauliflower - 1 (medium sized).

Bread - 6 slices

Finely cut onions - ¼ cup.

Chopped coriander
leaves - 1 Tbl. sp.

Bengal gram flour - 2 Tbl. sps.
(Besan)

Salt - as required

Fine bread crumbs - 2 Tbl. sps.

Cumin seeds - 1 tsp.

Poppy seeds - 1 Tbl. sp.

Cardamom - 2

Garlic - 2 flakes.

Cloves - 2

Red chillies - 7

Oil - for frying.

(Or)

Skewers for baking.

Method:-

1. Wash and cut cauliflower into big flowerettes.
2. Arrange on a sieve and steam for 3 minutes in cooker.
3. Cook dhal in enough water till one whistle sound.
4. Drain water completely.
5. Dry roast poppy and cumin separately.
6. Grind it along with red chillies, garlic, cardamom and cloves with minimum water possible.
7. Then add dhal, cauliflower and grind coarsely.
8. Heat oil in a pan and fry onions till crisp.
9. Add ground masala paste and fry till moisture dries up.
10. Dip bread slices in water and squeeze immediately to remove water. Add salt, chopped corriander, bengal gram flour to the paste.
11. Knead well and shape into Kababs.
12. Apply oil to skewers and shape a thin layer of paste on top.
13. Top with little butter and bake in pre heated oven till brown. (Tilt skewers while baking for even roasting).
14. Slice into 3 or 4 pieces and serve with vinegar onions.

Note:

Instead of using oven, this can be deep fried like other Kababs.

*Vinegar Onions:

Slice white onions into thin long pieces. Add salt, pepper, little sugar and malt vinegar. Mix well and keep aside for ½ an hour before serving.

44. VEGETABLE CUTLET

Ingredients:

Potatoes - ½ kg.

Big Onions - 2

Medium sized carrots - 4

Beetroot - 2

Shelled peas - ½ cup

Fine bread crumbs

(or)

Rusk powder - ½ cup.

Maida - 2 Tablespoons.

Salt - as required.

Red chilli powder - 1½ tsp.

Garam masala powder - ½ tsp.

Oil - enough for frying.

Method:-

1. Peel and chop onions finely.
2. Pressure cook potatoes with skin. Peel and mash coarsely.
3. Steam whole carrots and beetroot with peas on top container of pressure cookerr.
4. When it cools down grate carrots and beetroot.
5. Heat oil in a deep curved pan.
6. Fry onions till transparent.
7. Add grated vegetables mashed potatoes and peas.
8. Fry in a high flame till moisture is absorbed.
9. Sprinkle salt, chilli powder, garam masala and mix well. Remove from fire.
10. Allow to cool down completely.
11. Mix maida with little water and make into paste.
12. Make medium sized balls from fried vegetable mixture.
13. Dip it in maida paste and roll on bread crumbs to coat it well.
14. Shape as you like into thin cutlets.
15. Heat a 'tawa' and arrange few cutlets on top.
16. Pour oil around and fry till brown on both sides by turning it once.
17. Serve hot with tomato ketchup and mint chutney.

45.   SPICY CUTLET

Ingredients:

Potatoes - ½ kg.
Shelled Peas - ½ Cup
French beans - 100 gms.
Carrots - ¼ kg.
Cabbage - 200 gms.
Bread - 6 slices.
Fine bread crumbs
(dry) - ½ cup.
Onions - 2
Ginger, greenchilli
paste - 2 tsps.
Salt - as required
Garam masala
powder - ¾ tsp.
Corn flour - 1 Tbl.sp.
Oil - enough for frying.

Method:-

1. Dice Onions, Carrots, Cabbage, and beans as fine as possible.
2. Pressure cook potatoes with skin and steam all the other vegetables.
3. Peel skin from potatoes and mash well when it is still warm.
4. Heat oil in a deep curved pan and fry ginger chilli paste and then onions till crisp.
5. Stir in cooked vegetables, mashed potatoes and fry till dry.
6. Add salt, garam masala powder and remove from fire. Cool thoroughly.
7. Dip bread slices one by one quickly in water and squeeze well.
8. Add squeezed bread, Corn flour and half on the bread crumbs to the vegetable mixture.
9. Mix well with hands.
10. Make into balls and dredge on fine bread crumbs.
11. Shape into thin cutlets and fry on a hot 'tawa' with enough oil till crisp and brown on both sides. Serve' hot.

Note:

1. Half Cashewnut can be pressed down on each cutlet while shaping it.
2. Slice Onions into rings, tomatoes into thin rounds. Slice half boiled carrots and beetroots. Decorate all these around cutlets while serving.

46.   BEETROOT CUTLETS

Ingredients:

Potatoes - ½ kg.

Beetroot - 3
(Medium sized)

Big onions - 2

Ginger Garlic paste - 1 tsp.

Minced green chillies - 1 tsp.

Ani seed - ½ tsp.
(Sombu)

Red chilli powder - 1½ tsp.

Garam Masala Powder - ¾ tsp.

Salt - as required.

Dhania Powder - 1 tsp.

Dry Mango Powder - ½ tsp.

Fine bread crumbs - ½ cup (dry)

Oil - for frying.

Method:-

1. Pressure cook potatoes. Peel and mash well.
2. Peel outer skin from beetroot and steam it in pressure cooker without chopping (7 minutes).
3. After cooking grate beetroots.
4. Heat oil in a deep pan, add ani seed, ginger garlic paste, minced chillies and then onion.
5. Fry for few minutes and then add dhania powder, garam masala powder and chilli powder.
6. Continue frying with grated beetroots till moisture evaporates.
7. Add cooked mashed potatoes and salt.
8. Fry for few more minutes, add mango powder and remove from fire.
9. Allow to cool down and mix half of the bread crumbs to this.
10. Make balls and shape into thin cutlets.
11. Use other half of the bread crumbs for coating.
12. Fry on a hot 'tawa' using enough oil for frying till golden brown. Serve hot.

47. ALOO TIKKI

Ingredients:

Potatoes - 1 kg.

Peas - ¼ kg.

(Or)

Cauliflower - 1

Tomatoes - 3

Finely chopped onions - ¼ cup.

Bread - 1 loaf.

Mint leaves - 1 small bunch

Coriander leaves - 1 small bunch.

Salt - as required.

Red Chilli powder - 2 tsps.

Garam masala

powder - 1 tsp.

Oil - for frying.

Method:-

1. Pressure cook potatoes.
2. Peel and mash well without any lumps when it is still warm.
3. Dip bread slices one by one in water, squeeze well and add to potatoes.
4. Add salt, chilli powder, garam masala, chopped mint, coriander leaves and mix well like a dough.
5. Cook peas separately.
6. Blanch tomatoes in hot water, remove skin and grind to a Soft pulp. Strain well.
7. Heat little oil, add cumin seed and onion.
8. Fry till crisp, add tomato pulp, salt, little red chilli powder, garam masala powder and cooked peas.
9. Cook till dry and remove from fire. [This is used as stuffing.]
10. Make even sized balls from potato dough. Make a dent and keep little 'peas' stuffing inside.
11. Seal well on all sides properly.
12. Flatten the tikkis and shallow fry with liberal oil till crisp and brown on both sides.
13. Serve with sweet chutney, finely chopped onions, mint chutney, tomato sauce (or) channa masala.
[Recipe given at the end of this book.]

Note:

These tikkis can be deep fried in hot oil till crisp.

Variations:

1. Soak whole green gram in water for few hours. Cook till one whistle in cooker. Make stuffing as mentioned previously instead of peas or cauliflower.
2. Omit red chilli powder. Add ginger, green chilli paste with a Tbl sp. of coriander to the boiled potatoes and make tikkis.

48.   CHEESE CUTLETS

Ingredients:

Potatoes - ½ kg.

Onions - 2 big

Capsicums - 2

Cabbage - 150 gms

Green chillies - 7

Ginger Garlic paste - ½ tsp.

Cooking cheese grated - ½ cup.

Powdered salt - as required.

Garam masala

powder - ½ tsp.

Oil - for frying.

Bread crumbs (or) Rusk

powder - ½ cup.

Maida - 3 Tbl.sp.

Method:-

1. Pressure cook potatoes. Peel and mash well.
2. Grate onions and cabbage.
3. Chop Capsicum into fine pieces. Mince green chillies.
4. Heat oil in a deep pan and add ½ teaspoon of cumin seed or ani seed.
5. Add ginger garlic paste, minced chillies and then onion.
6. When it is half fried add grated cabbage and capsicum.
7. Stir constantly till raw smell goes in reduced flame.
8. Add mashed potatoes, salt, garam masala and fry for few minutes.
9. Remove from fire and cool down thoroughly.
10. Add grated cheese and half of the bread crumbs.
11. Mix well and make into balls.
12. Dip in maida paste and roll on bread crumbs.
13. Fry on hot 'tawa' till crisp with enough oil on both sides.

Note:

If cutlets looses its shape while frying add few soaked, squeezed bread slices to the potato mixture.

* Cooking cheese gives best results than ordinary cheese cubes.

49. GREEN CUTLETS

Ingredients:

Bengal gram dhal - 1 cup.

Onions - 3

Amaranth greens - 2 bunches

(Mulai Keerai)

Ginger, green chilli

paste - 2 teaspoons.

Bread slices - 10

Dry bread crumbs - 5 Tbl.sp.

Corn flour - 2 Tbl.sp.

Garam masala

powder - 1 tsp.

Lemon - 1

Salt - as required.

Oil - for frying.

Method:-

1. Pressure cook bengal gram dhal in just enough water for one whistle sound.
2. Drain excess water and grind dhal to coarse paste. (or) mash well when it is still warm.
3. Chop onions and greens to fine pieces.
4. Heat oil in a deep pan and fry ginger chilli paste and then onions.
5. When it becomes transparent add greens and fry well raw smell goes.
6. Add mashed dhal and fry till dry.
7. Mix salt and garam masala powder. Squeeze lime and and remove from fire.
8. Dip bread slices one by one in water and squeeze excess moisture.
9. Add squeezed bread, half of the dry bread crumbs and corn flour to the fried dhal paste.
10. Knead well and make medium sized balls.
11. Flatten and shape into thin cutlets, using rest of the bread crumbs for coating.
12. Fry on a hot 'tawa' with enough oil till crisp and brown on both sides.

Note:

Whenever making any type of cutlet keep them in refrigerator for atleast ½ an hour before frying which gives good results.

50. SAGO CUTLETS

Ingredients:

Potatoes - ½ kg

Sago - ½ cup.

Bread - 6 slices.

Dry bread crumbs - 4 Tbl. sps.

Garam Masala Powder - ½ tsp.

Salt - as required

Oil - for frying

Finely cut onions - 3 Tbl. sps.

Coarsely powdered pea
nuts - 2 Tbl.sps.

Red chilli powder - ½ tsp.

Grind to paste:

Green chillies - 5

Ginger - ½ inch piece.

Coriander leaves - 1 Tbl.sp.

Curry leaves - 1 Tbl.sp.

Mint leaves - 1 Tbl.sp.

Salt - a pinch.

Method:-

1. Pressure cook potatoes. Peel and mash well.
2. Soak sago in just enough water for one hour.
3. Heat little oil in a frying pan.
4. Add ani seeds and then ground paste.
5. Fry for a minute and then mix onions.
6. Stir for few minutes and then add potatoes.
7. Sprinkle salt, garam masala powder, chilli powder and remove from fire.
8. Dip bread slices one by one in water and squeeze well.
9. Add this to the potato mixture with pea nut powder, half of the bread crumbs and sago.
10. Shape into cutlets using other half of bread crumbs for dredging.
11. Shallow fry on hot frying pan with enough oil for both sides.

51. BANANA CUTLETS

Ingredients:

Raw bananas - 2
(Plantain)
Potatoes - ¼ kg.
Onions - 2
Coriander leaves - 1 small bunch.
Ginger - ¼ inch piece.
Green chillies - 4
Red chilli powder - ½ tsp.
Salt as required.
Garam masala powder - 1 tsp.
'Am chur' - 1 tsp.
(Dry Mango powder)
Pepper powder - ¼ tsp.
Oil - for frying
Fine bread crumbs - 3 Tbl.Sps.
Maida - 1 Tbl.Sp.
Corn flour - 2 Tbl.Sps.

Method:-

1. Pressure cook potatoes. Peel and mash well.
2. Steam banana's with skin in pressure cooker till one whistle sound.
3. Cool down, Peel skin and grate it.
4. Dice onions and chillies finely.
5. Heat oil in a frying pan, add cumin seed, crushed ginger and chillies.
6. Fry for a minute and add onions.
7. Stir for 2 to 3 minutes and then mix grated banana.
8. Fry well till it turns light brown.
9. Add mashed potatoes salt, Chilli powder, pepper powder, garam masala and chopped coriander leaves.
10. Remove from fire and mix dry mango powder, maida and half of the bread crumbs. Knead well like a dough.
11. Make balls and dust with corn flour and bread crumbs.
12. Shallow fry with enough oil.

VARIATIONS:

Brinjal Cutlet:

Roast brinjals with skin on direct flame till it turns dark in colour. (or) Pressure cook whole brinjals in separate vessel without adding water for 15 minutes. Peel and mash well. Omit bananas in previous recipe and follow the recipe with brinjals. Sprinkle little tamarind water instead of Am chur. Omit pepper powder. Add few soaked and squeezed bread slices.

Paneer Cutlets:

Knead crumbled paneer with little rice flour and maida. Add cooked potatoes, fried onions and other spices as per taste and make cutlets.

Corn Potato Tikkis:

Grind cooked corn with green chillies and coriander leaves to coarse paste, without adding water. Fry cumin seeds, onions, shredded cabbage and then ground corn, mashd potatoes. Add other seasonings and make cutlets.

Rawa Cutlets:

Using cooked potatoes as binding agent add roasted rawa, finely chopped fried onions and greens. Use other seasonings as per taste as mentioned in previous recipes, and make cutlets.

Sprouted green gram Cutlets:

Steam sprouted gram for 2 minutes. Grind coarsely. Fry with onions, tomatoes, ginger garlic paste, chilli paste and other spices. Add cooked potatoes, bread slices and make thin cutlets.

Vermicelli Cutlets:

Make mixed vegetable cutlets as in recipe No. 45. Roast crushed vermicelli in little ghee. Dip the cutlets in bengal gram flour paste and then dust with vermicelli. Shape and fry on a hot tawa.

52. VEGETABLE SIZZLERS

Ingredients:

Vegetables:

Onion - 2

Tomatoes - 2 or 3

Cucumber - 150 gms.

Carrot - 2

Cabbage - 150 gms

Peas - 100 gms

Capsicums - 2 (Medium sized)

Spring onions - optional.

Sauces:

Worcestershire sauce.

Tomato sauce.

Chilli sauce.

Cutlets - few.

Vinegar - 2 Tbl.sps.

Butter - 100 gms

Iron pan - Medium thickness.

Or

'tawa'

Grind together:

Red chillies - 6

Garlic - 3 flakes.

Mustard - ¼ tsp.

Salt - ¼ tsp.

Method:-

1. Par boil whole carrots, Cabbage leaves (3 inch square pieces) and shelled peas in water for 2 minutes. Strain well.

2. Slice onions, Capsicums, tomatoes, cucumber into thin discs.

3. Cut par boiled vegetables into discs and prick with a fork.

4. Smear ground paste on all vegetables.

5. Heat half of the butter in a pan and fry the vegetables carefully without mashing it.

6. Heat a flat 'tawa' and arrange cut lets in the Centre and other vegetables around carefully in decorative manner.

7. Sprinkle all the sauces as per taste and other half of the butter.

8. Finally keeping yourself little away from the hot pan, sprinkle vinegar on top.

9. Bring hot to the table with the 'tawa' and serve sizzling hot.

Caution:

Butter and vinegar together added to hot pan gives sizzler effects with splutter sounds.

Note:

In the above recipe instead of slicing tomatoes and capsicums stuff them with mixed rice (or) vegetable masala. Select firm red tomatoes and small capsicums. Slice top and carefully scoop out centres. Stuff with cooked rice which is mixed with salt, chilli powder, tomato sauce and chilli sauce. Close and keep under grill for few minutes. Arrange next to cutlets in the above recipe.

53. VEGETABLE BURGERS

Ingredients:

Prepared vegetable cutlets - 6
Round buns - 6
Cabbage - 150 gms
Onions - 2
Tomatoes - 2
Beetroot - 2
Tomato sauce - as required.
Grated cheese - Optional.
Butter - 50 gms.

Method:-

1. Make spicy thin vegetable cutlets into round shape and fry till crisp.
2. Cut bun diagonally into two and apply butter.
3. Separate cabbage leaves and blanch in hot water (to which little salt and turmeric powder is added) for 5 minutes. Strain water and wipe the leaves.
4. Cut onions and tomatoes into thin discs.
5. Peel beetroot and blanch in hot water. Slice thinly.
6. Heat a tawa and lightly toast bun both sides.
7. Arrange one or two cabbage leaves and a piece of onion, one cutlet, one tomato piece and beetroot as layers in between bun.
8. Pierce with tooth pick and serve with sauce.
9. If grated cheese is added bake in a hot oven for 2 minutes for cheese to melt.

Note:

Sprinkle little salt, pepper and little lime juice (or) vinegar over vegetable pieces before arranging.

54. SAGO BONDA

Ingredients:

Sago - 1 cup.

Rice flour - ½ cup.

Thick, sour curds - 1 cup.

Soaked bengal gram

dhal - 1 Tbl.sp.

Finely cut onions - ¼ cup.

Minced green chillies - 2 tsps

Salt - as required.

Oil - to deep fry.

Method:-

1. Wash sago and drain water completely.
2. Add whipped curds, salt and mix well.
3. Allow it to soak for atleast 6 hours.
4. Just before frying add rice flour, soaked dhal, chillies, onion and mix well. If necessary add some more curds, or rice flour.
5. Make balls and deep fry in hot oil till crisp and brown.
6. Remove Bondas from pan and put in a strainer for few minutes to drain excess oil. Serve with any pickle.

Note:

Only sour thick curds should be added. Do not add water at all which makes the bonda to splutter while frying. Curds can be adjusted as per size of the sago. 8 to 10 bondas can be deep fried at a time or till the oil holds. While frying do not disturb with laddle till it turns its colour underneath.

Variations:

1. **Sago vada:** Add little more rice flour, chopped cashews and flatten like vadas. Deep fry in hot oil.
2. Mix equal measures of rawa, maida, sago, rice flour in curds. Make bondas as mentioned in the above recipe.

55.   VEGETABLE BONDA

Ingredients:

For the batter:

Bengal gram flour - 1 cup.
Rice flour - $\frac{1}{3}$ cup.
Salt - as required.
Red chilli powder - $\frac{3}{4}$ tsp.
Cooking soda - 2 pinches.

For the filling:

Finely cut onions - $\frac{1}{2}$ cup.
Mixed diced vegetables - 3 cups.
(Potatoes, beans, carrots, cauli-
flower, beetroot etc.)
Shelled peas - $\frac{1}{4}$ cup.
Ginger garlic paste - $\frac{1}{2}$ tsp.
Minced green chillies - $1\frac{1}{2}$ tsp.
Salt - as required.
Chopped coriander leaves - 2 Tbl.
                                    sps.
Turmeric powder - $\frac{1}{4}$ tsp.
Oil - for frying.
Lemon - 1.

Method:

1. Steam vegetables in pressure cooker.
2. Drain well after cooking to remove excess moisture.
3. Heat oil in a frying pan, add ginger garlic paste and then onions.
4. Fry for few minutes and then add minced chillies, turmeric, cooked vegetables and salt.
5. Stir in a high flame till moisture is absorbed completely.
6. Squeeze lemon and add coriander leaves and remove from fire.
7. When cools down make medium sized balls.
8. Mix all the ingredients as mentioned and prepare a thick batter by mixing with water.
9. Dip the balls one by one in the batter and put in hot oil. (Few at a time).
10. Deep fry till golden brown.

56. ALOO BONDA

Ingredients:

For stuffing:

Cooked potatoes - ½ kg.
Finely cut onions - ½ cup.
Minced green chillies - 2 tsps.
Powdered salt - as required.
Chopped coriander leaves - 3 Tbl.
sps.
Lemon - 1.

Method:

1. Peel outer skin from cooked potatoes.
2. Mash well when it is still warm.
3. Add all the other ingredients and mix well. Squeeze lime.
4. Make balls, dip in the batter and deep fry as mentioned in previous recipe.

Variation:

Make a masala with fried onions, cooked peas and potatoes with seasonings. Make balls, dip in batter and deep fry.

To avoid worms (or) other pests in dhal or
rice keep neem leaves in that container.

---

57. MYSORE BONDA

Ingredients:

Dehusked black gram - 1 cup.
Red gram dhal - 1 Tbl. sp.
(Thuar)
Oil - To deep fry.
Green chillies - 12.
Ginger - 1 inch piece.
Finely chopped coconut - 2 Tbl. sps.
Salt - as required.

Powder coarsely:

Pepper - 1 tsp.
Cumin seeds - ½ tsp.

Method:

1. Soak dhal in water for 3 hours.
2. Drain water and grind to smooth frothy paste. Add salt. (with minimum water possible).
3. Chop chillies and ginger to fine pieces.
4. Mix other ingredients to the dhal paste.
5. Make balls using wet hands and put directly in hot oil.
6. Deep fry till golden brown and serve with chutney.

When pans are badly burned and crusted,
fill them with soapy water and let it boil for
15 minutes. This will help to remove burnt
marks while washing.

---

58. PULLANI VUNTA

Ingredients:

Raw rice - 1 cup.

Black gram - ⅓ cup.
(dehusked)

Salt - as required.

Soaked bengal gram dhal - 1 Tbl.
sp.

Finely cut onions - ¼ cup.

Green chillies - 10.
(Chop or mince)

Oil - to deep fry.

Finely cut coriander leaves - 1 Tbl.
sp.

Method:

1. Soak rice and dhal together in enough water.
2. Grind to smooth and frothy paste with salt. (Thicker than dosa dough).
3. Allow it to become sour. (Keep for 2 days in warm place).
4. Mix all the other ingredients.
5. Drop spoonsfull in hot oil.
6. Fry till golden and serve with chutney or pickle.

Note:

Any left over dosa batter from previous day's can be used to prepare this. If batter is watery soak little sago in the batter itself (1 or 2 Tbl. spoon) for 5 to 6 hours. Then deep fry like other bondas.

59. MANGALORE BONDA

Ingredients:

Maida - 1 cup.

Rice flour - ¼ cup.

Rawa - 1 Tbl. sp.

Finely cut onions - ¼ cup.

Minced green chillies - 1 Tbl. sp.

Finely chopped coriander, curry leaves - 2 Tbl. sps.

Cooking soda - a pinch.

Salt - as required.

Thick, sour curds - 1 cup.

Method:

1. Mix all the ingredients together in a bowl.
2. Keep closed for atleast 5 to 6 hours. (Add soda just before frying).
3. Heat oil in a deep curved pan.
4. By using wet hands make medium sized balls and put in the oil.
5. Deep fry till golden brown and serve hot.

Note:

Do not over fry the bondas which changes its taste. Use just required curds to hold the dough. Do not add water.

Variation:

1. Equal measures of rice flour, rawa and maida also can be used to make bondas.
2. Rawa alone can be soaked in curds to make bondas.
3. Add chopped greens or finely cut vegetables to the dough just before frying.

60. CHEESE BONDA

Ingredients:

Maida - 1 cup.
Grated cheese - ½ cup.
(cooking cheese)
Chopped cashewnuts - 1 Tbl. sp.
Finely cut coriander and curry
leaves - 2 Tbl. sps.
Salt - as required.
Minced green chillies - 1 Tbl. sp.
Water - for mixing the dough.
Oil - to deep fry.

Method:

1. Mix all the ingredients together in a bowl.
2. Add just enough water to hold the dough and mix well, without lumps.
3. Keep closed for ½ an hour.
4. Make balls and deep fry like other bondas.

Variations:

Bread cheese balls: Crumble fresh bread into fine pieces. (Crust removed). Soak in just enough milk. Add grated cheese, little maida, salt, baking powder, chopped onions, chillies, coriander leaves and make balls. Deep fry like other bondas.

Note: This bonda should be fried immediately after mixing. Use 'cooking cheese' only for best results. If bonda looses its shape while frying add dry bread crumbs (or) corn flour along with maida.

61. PALAK DUMPLINGS

Ingredients:

Green gram dhal - 1 cup.
(dehusked, split)
Chopped palak leaves - ¾ cup.
(spinach)
Finely cut onions - ¼ cup.
Chopped green chillies - 1 Tbl. sp.
Baking powder - a pinch.
Salt - as required.
Oil - for deep frying.

Method:

1. Soak dhal in water for 3 to 4 hours.
2. Drain water completely and grind to smooth frothy paste without adding water.
3. Add salt, other ingredients, and mix gently.
4. Do not over stir.
5. Deep fry in hot oil by making small balls with hands (or) drop spoonsfull directly in oil.
6. Serve hot.

Variations:

1. Omit palak. Use any other greens.
2. Add crushed ginger along with minced chillies to the batter.

62. RIDGE GOURD DUMPLINGS

Ingredients:

Bengal gram flour - 1 cup.
Ridge gourd - 2 or 3.
Red chilli powder - ½ tsp.
Green chilli paste - ½ tsp.
Salt - as required.
Cooking soda (or) baking
                 powder - a pinch.
Oil - for frying.

Method:

1. Peel the outer skin from gourd and chop into fine pieces. (Check for bitterness).
2. Mix with flour and other dry ingredients.
3. Divide into portions and add water each time separately before deep frying. (As oil holds).

4. Drop spoonsfull in oil as mentioned in previous recipe.
5. When golden, remove from fire and serve hot.

Variations:

1. Finely chopped onions can be added along with this.
2. Any other chopped greens, cashewnuts can be added to the flour to make this recipe.

63. MINT PAKODAS

Ingredients:

Bengal gram dhal - 1 cup.
Finely chopped fresh mint
                leaves - 1 cup.
Chopped coriander leaves - ⅓ cup.
Salt - as required.
Oil - to deep fry.

Make into paste:

Ginger - 1 inch piece.
Green chillies - 10 to 12.

Method:

1. Soak dhal for 2 hours in water.
2. Drain water completely.
3. Grind very coarsely with salt.
4. Add ground paste, mint leaves, coriander leaves and mix well.
5. Make into medium sixed balls and deep fry in hot oil till crisp.

To clean dials on stoves and other hard to reach surfaces in any glass ornamental ware use a cotton swab dipped in liquid detergent.

64. POTATO NEST

Ingredients:

Cooked potatoes - ½ kg.
Finely cut onions - 2 Tbl. sps.
Cooked peas - ½ cup.
Broken vermicelli - 1 cup.
Salt - as required.
Red chilli powder - 1½ tsp.
Green chilli paste - 1 tsp.
Coriander leaves - 2 Tbl. sps.
Garam masala powder - ¼ tsp.
Oil - for frying.

Make into paste:

Maida - 1 Tbl. sp.
Corn flour - 1 Tbl. sp.
Water - ¼ cup.

Method:

1. Peel outer skin from cooked potatoes and mash well without any lumps.
2. Add salt, red chilli powder, chilli paste, ground coriander leaves and mix well.
3. Heat little oil and fry onions till crisp.
4. Add cooked peas salt, little chilli powder and garam masala.
5. Fry till moisture is absorbed and remove from fire.
6. Make medium sized balls from potato mixture.
7. Make a dent and keep little peas stuffing inside.
8. Close and seal well properly.
9. Shape like an egg, dip in Maida paste and roll on vermicelli bits.
10. Chill for ½ an hour.
11. Deep fry in hot oil till crisp and brown.
12. Just before serving cut them diagonally and arrange on a plate of coriander leaves or cabbage leaves.
13. Serve with tomato ketchup.

Note:

For best results use half cooked vermicelli bits which is dried well by spreading over a towel.

73

65. GARAM PAKODAS

Ingredients:

Bengal gram flour - 1 cup.
Rice flour - 1 cup.
Ghee - 2 Tbl. sps.
Cooking soda - a pinch.
Onions - 3 or 4.
Green chillies - 4.
Salt - as required.
Chopped curry, coriander
        leaves - 3 Tbl. sps.
Oil - for deep frying.
Red chilli powder - 1 tsp.

Method:

1. Sieve both rice flour and gram flour together with salt and chilli powder.
2. In a broad basin rub ghee with a pinch of soda, till it forms a frothy paste.
3. Mix flour to this and blend well with finger tips till ghee is equally dispersed in flour.
4. Add other ingredients and mix well.
5. Heat oil in a deep curved pan.
6. Divide the flour to 5 or 6 portions.
7. To one portion sprinkle very little water just to hold flour.
8. Using finger tips crumble the prepared dough and put directly in hot oil. (irregular shape is formed).
9. Deep fry till crisp and brown.

Note:

Each time sprinkle water and mix separately, till the oil holds.

Variations:

1. **Medhu pakodas:** For softer pakodas reduce rice flour to ½ cup while mixing the dough. Little more water should be sprinkled which makes pakodas softer after frying.
2. **Cashewnut pakoda:** Omit onions. Add chopped cashewnuts and coriander leaves.
3. **Mint pakoda:** Omit onions. Add a cup of chopped mint leaves and coriander leaves and make pakodas. Crushed ginger can also be put in the dough before mixing with water.

66. PANEER PAKODAS

Ingredients:

Crumbled Paneer - 1 cup.

Bengal gram flour - ½ cup.

Rice flour - ¼ cup.

Onions (sliced lengthwise) - ½ cup.

Salt - as required.

Red chilli powder - ½ tsp.

Chopped cashewnuts - 1 Tbl. sp.

Finely cut coriander and mint
              leaves - 1 Tbl. sp.

Oil - Enough for frying.

Method:

1. Crumble paneer well without any lumps.
2. Mix with other dry ingredients.
3. Add two tablespoons of hot oil to that.
4. Mix well with onions.
5. Divide it into 3 or 4 parts.
6. Sprinkle very little water. (Only if necessary — because moisture in the paneer itself might hold the dough well).
7. Deep fry pakodas as mentioned in previous recipe.

When a recipe is doubled never double the salt and other seasonings. Use little more than mentioned. Taste and then add more if necessary.

67. BREAD PAKODAS

Ingredients:

Bengal gram flour - ¼ cup.
Rice flour - 1 Tbl. sp.
Onions - 2.
Ghee - 2 tsps.
Cooking soda - a pinch.
Green chillies - 2.
Chopped mint leaves - 1 Tbl. sp.
Red chilli powder - ¼ tsp.
Cashewnuts - 1 Tbl. sp.
Bread slices - 8.
Sour butter milk - 2 tsps.
Oil - for frying.

Method:

1. Slice onions and chillies lengthwise.
2. Remove crusts from bread slices and crumble coarsely.
3. Sprinkle butter milk to this. Keep aside for ½ an hour.
4. Rub ghee and soda in a basin till frothy.
5. Add all the ingredients and mix well.
6. Sprinkle very little water if necessary.
7. Make pakodas as mentioned in previous recipes and deep fry till crisp. Serve hot.

68. VERMICELLI PAKODAS

Ingredients:

Onions - 3.
Vermicelli - 1 cup.
Cooked potato - 1.
Ginger garlic paste - 1 tsp.
Green chillies - 6.
Salt - as required.
Bengal gram flour - ¼ cup.
Rice flour - 1 Tbl. sp.
Chopped coriander
          leaves - 1 Tbl. sp.
Red chilli powder - ½ tsp.
Mint leaves, cashewnuts
             - Optional.
Oil - for deep frying.

Method:

1. Slice onions and chillies lengthwise.
2. Roast vermicelli till golden. Pour hot water and cook till just soft.
3. Drain water well. Add little more cold water and drain well through colander.
4. Mash the potatoes.
5. Mix with vermicelli and other ingredients. (Do not add water).
6. Add a table spoon of hot oil and mix lightly.
7. Deep fry in hot oil like other pakodas.

Note: Apply little melted ghee to Vermicelli bits. Then roast it in a hot deep frying pan in medium flame stirring constatly.

BAJJI VARIETIES

69. ONION BAJJI

Ingredients:

For Basic Bajji Batter:

Bengal gram flour - 1 cup.
Rice flour - ½ cup.
Maida - 1 Tbl. sp.
Salt - as required.
Red chilli powder - 1 tsp.
Cooking soda - 2 pinches.
Oil - to deep fry.
Onions - 6 or 7.

Method:

1. Select medium sized onions.
2. Peel outer skin and slice into thin rounds.
3. Arrange on a plate carefully without separating the rings.
4. Mix all the dry ingredients in bowl.
5. Pour water gradually and mix the flour without forming lumps till the batter reaches dropping consistency.
6. Heat oil in a deep curved pan.
7. When it smokes, dip onion slices one by one in the batter to coat both sides and slip in oil carefully. (8 to 10 pieces can be fried at a time (or) till the oil holds).
8. When it turns golden turn over and cook till done.
9. Drain excess oil on a colander (or) absorbant paper and serve hot.

Note: To obtain crisp bajjis, omit maida and add more rice flour. Do not add more soda which makes the bajji to consume more oil.

Variations: Bajjis can be made with following vegetables, using the same batter.

1. Boiled potatoes which is sliced into thin rounds.
2. Peeled raw bananas (plantain) which is sliced thinly lengthwise.
3. Brinjals sliced into rounds.
4. Half cooked cauliflower pieces.
5. Bread slices which is cut into medium squares.

78

6. Capsicum sliced into broad squares.
7. Snake gourd cut into rectangles.
8. Stuffed green chillies, stuffed potatoes etc.
9. Palak leaf (spinach).
10. Sliced onions or cashewnuts or peanuts can be mixed with little batter just to coat that and deep fried like pakoras.

11. **Maida Bajjis:**

Try this when bengal gram flour is not available at home. Mix little melted ghee or butter with maida, salt and blend well. Add red chilli powder, water and make a thick batter. Keep closed for 3 to 4 hours. Mix a pinch of soda just before frying. Dip slices of vegetables in this batter and deep fry like other bajjis.

To prevent worms in rawa dry roast it in a deep curved pan over medium flame till it becomes warm. Cool down and preserve in air tight containers.

70. LAYERED SANDWICH BAJJI

Ingredients:

Bread - 1 loaf.
Bajji Batter - as required.
(Refer previous recipe)
Tomato chutney - ¼ cup.
Mint chutney - ¼ cup.
Butter - 100 gms.
Oil - for deep frying.

Mint chutney:

Grind together:

Mint leaves - 1 cup.
Chopped coriander leaves - ½ cup.
Green chillies - 4.
Ginger - small piece.
Cumin seeds - ½ tsp.
Tamarind - little.
Salt - as required.
Onion - ½.
Grated Coconut - 2 Tbl. sps.

Method:

1. Trim brown crusts from bread slices.
2. Apply butter to one side of all slices.
3. To one slice apply 1 tsp. of mint chutney on top of butter.
4. Keep another slice on top. (buttered side up).
5. Apply 1 tsp. of tomato chutney and seal with another slice of bread. (3 slices on top of the other).
6. Make all the slices in the same manner.
7. Cut each block into 4 square pieces.
8. Dip in bajji batter to coat it well and deep fry in hot oil till crisp and brown.

* Tomato chutney – Refer next page.

* Tomato Chutney:

Ingredients:

Cloves - 2.
Cinnamon - 1 inch piece.
Garlic - 5 flakes.
Chopped onions - ½ cup.
Chopped tomatoes - 1 cup.
Turmeric powder - ¼ tsp.
Salt - as required.
Red chilli powder - ½ tsp.

Method:

1. Fry masala spices and then onions till crisp in oil (or) ghee
2. Add tomatoes and fry till moisture is absorbed.
3. Mix other ingredients and remove from fire.
4. Grind to smooth paste.

Note:

Tomato ketchup and chilli sauce can be used instead of chutney in the above recipe.

Line the jar in which salt is kept with blotting paper to keep it dry always.

71. DEEP FRIED LADIES FINGERS

Ingredients:

Ladies fingers - ¼ kg.
Oil - for deep frying.
Tamarind - gooseberry sized.
Turmeric powder - ¼ tsp.
Salt - as required.
Bread crumbs - ½ cup.

For the batter:

Bengal gram flour - ½ cup.
Rice flour - ¼ cup.
Salt - ½ tsp.
Red chilli powder - ½ tsp.
Dhania powder - 1 tsp.
Cooking soda - a pinch.
Garam masala powder - ¼ tsp.

Method:

1. Trim edges from the tender ladies fingers.
2. Heat 2 cups of water with tamarind, salt and turmeric powder.
3. Put ladies fingers in that when it starts boiling.
4. After two minutes drain water well and wipe ladies fingers with a towel.
5. Mix mentioned ingredients for the batter with just enough water.
6. Dip ladies fingers in the batter and roll on bread crumbs.
7. Deep fry in hot oil till crisp and brown. Serve hot.

72. CAPSICUM BAJJI

Ingredients:

Small capsicums - ½ kg.
Bengal gram flour - 1½ cups.
Rice flour - ½ cup.
Salt - 1 tsp.
Red chilli powder - 1 tsp.
Cooking soda - 2 pinches.
Oil - to deep fry.

For garnishing:

Finely chopped onions - ½ cup.
Lemon - 1.
Salt and chilli powder - as per taste.

Method:

1. Make bajji batter with gram flour, rice flour, salt, chilli powder and soda by mixing with just enough water.
2. Dip whole capsicums in this and deep fry in hot oil till golden brown.
3. After removing from fire cut the capsicums in the centre with sharp knife.
4. Stuff with onions, salt and chilli powder. Squeeze lemon and serve immediately with *Sweet chutney.

*Sweet chutney: (Refer Pani puri).

> To keep dampness from affecting flour while it is stored, tuck a bay leaf inside the container. This helps to absorb the moisture.

73. STUFFED CHILLI BAJJI

Ingredients:

Green chillies - ¼ kg.
(long, thick, Bajji variety).
Oil - for deep frying.

For stuffing:

Grated dry coconut - 2 Tbl. sps.
Roasted gram - 1½ Tbl. sp.
(chutney dhal)
Tamarind - little.
Salt - as required.
Omam (or) Cumin seeds - ½ tsp.
(Powder all the ingredients and
mix with finely cut onions).

For garnishing:

Finely cut onions - ½ cup.
Lemon - 1 or 2.
Sweet chutney - ¼ cup.

For Bajji batter:

Bengal gram flour - 2 cups.
Rice flour - ¼ cup.
Maida - 1 Tbl. sp.
Salt & Chilli powder - as per taste.
Cooking soda - 2 pinches.
Sweet chutney - Refer (Pani puri)
     (Page No. 9)

Method:

1. Slit the chilli carefully and remove the seeds inside using a sharp knife.
2. Stuff a table spoon of powdered ingredients carefully inside.
3. Mix bajji batter little thicker than other normal batter.
4. Dip the stuffed chillies carefully in the batter and deep fry in hot oil till golden in colour.
5. To serve the chillies slit on top with a sharp knife lengthwise.
6. Put little finely cut onions, squeeze little lemon juice and top with sweet chutney.

Variations:

1. Slice the chillies into two breadwise if chillies are very long and do the recipe with the stuffing.

2. Slice the chillies lengthwise and remove the seeds. Apply little paste made with ginger, garlic, red chillies, chutney gram, tamarind, salt and jaggery. Deep fry after dipping in bajji batter.

3. If ordinary green chillies are used, after removing the seeds soak them in lemon juice for 3 (or) 4 hours.

74. LASANIA (Stuffed Potato Bajji)

Ingredients:

Bengal gram flour - 1 cup.
Turmeric powder - a pinch.
Red chilli powder - 1 tsp.
Dhania powder - 1 tsp.
Salt - as required.
Cooking soda - 2 pinches.
Oil - for deep frying.
Small potatoes - ¼ kg.

For stuffing:

Grind together:

Garlic - 4 flakes.
Red chilli powder - 3 tsps.
Cumin seeds - 1 tsp.
(Jeera)
Salt - 1½ tsp.

Method:

1. Pressure cook potatoes.
2. Peel outer skin and make a slit from top to ¾th of its depth.
3. Stuff with ground paste.
4. Mix gram flour, turmeric, soda, salt, dhania powder, chilli powder with water to make a batter of dropping consistency.
5. Dip potatoes in this batter and deep fry in hot oil.

Note: Select tiny baby potatoes for this recipe.

VADAI VARIETIES

This traditional snack is very common in Indian homes. This dish is prepared by griding different kinds of soaked pulses to which some cereal also added at times.

A stone grinder is generally used which gives best results, than a mixie. After grinding, the dhal paste is made into small balls and patted on top of a plastic sheet or on wet cloth to make it flat using wet hands. Make a hole in the centre and deep fry in hot oil till crisp and brown on both sides.

75.   MEDHU VADAI

Ingredients:

Dehusked black gram - 1 cup.
(whole)

Rock salt - 1 tsp.
(heaped)

Rice flour - 2 Tbl.sps.

Oil - enough for deep frying.

Method:

1. Soak dhal in enough water for 1½ to 2 hours.
2. Drain water completely and grind dhal to smooth, frothy paste without adding water. (Approximately 30 minutes in a normal grinder).
3. Add salt at the end of grinding. Mix rice flour with this.
4. Heat oil in a deep curved frying pan.
5. Using wet hands shape little dough into a ball and then pat on top of a platic sheet or wet muslin cloth.
6. Put a hole in the Centre.
7: Deep fry in hot oil. (Few vadais can be fried at a time in the oil). Do not disturb till underneath turns to golden colour. Turn once to fry the other side brown, and crisp.
8. Serve hot with idli and sambhar.

Note: Use the dough immediately after grinding. If kept in refrigerator for few hours add little more rice flour before frying, otherwise vadai consumes more oil. (¼ cup of Red gram dhal (thuar) can be added to one cup of black gram while soaking.)

Variations:

1. **Spicy Vadai:** Grind few green chilles, a pinch of asafoetida and little green chillies. Add this to the ground vadai mixture to make the vadai spicy.

2. **Onion Vadai:** After grinding dhal mix finely cut onions and green chillies. Make vadai as mentioned previously.

3. **Vegetable Vadai:** Chop onions, carrots, cabbage, french beans, coriander leaves into fine pieces. Mix this with minced green chillies to dhal paste and prepare vadai. (any one vegetable can also be used).

4. **Greens vadai:** Chop any kerai (greens) into fine pieces. Mix this along with cut onions and chillies to dhal paste and make vadai. (Arai keerai tastes better).

5. **Rasa vadai:** After deep frying the medhu vadai soak in hot rasam (dhal rasam) for one (or) two hours before serving.

6. **Sambhar vadai:** Make onion sambhar. Soak the deep fried onion vadai in sambhar for 2 or 3 hours. Serve topped with little more sambhar and finely cut raw onions.

76.   THAIR VADAI

Ingredients:

Black gram dhal - 1 cup.
   (de husked)

Salt - 1 tsp.

Oil - for deep frying.

Fresh thick curds - 3 cups.

Grind together:

Grated fresh coconut - 2 Tbl sps.

Cashewnuts - 8

Green chillies - 8 to 10

Salt - as required.

Method:

1. Soak dhal in enough water for 2 hours.
2. Grind and deep fry vadais as given in previous recipe.
3. Whip curds and add ground paste to that.
4. Keep the curds in a broad vessel.
5. After deep frying the vadai dip it in warm water, lift out immediately.
6. Put the vadais in prepared curds and allow it to soak for 2 to 3 hours.
7. Just before serving arrange on a plate with more curds on top. Garnish as you like.

Garnish I: Sprinkle fried boondhi (Made of Bengal gram flour), finely chopped coriander leaves and curry leaves.

Garnish II: Soak vadai in plain whipped curds. Sprinkle powdered 'Kala namak', roasted jeera powder, plain salt and little chilli powder just before serving.

Note: Thair vadai must be consumed within 10 to 12 hours or they may become sour.

Variations:

1. **Stuffed thair vadai:**
   a. Mix fresh grated coconut, finely cut cashewnuts, almonds, raisins, tutty fruity pieces together. Stuff little of this mixture inside each vadai while making. They deep fry. soak in curds as mentioned previously and serve.
   b. Mix finely chopped green chillies, ginger and assorted chopped nuts. While making vadai, pat little dough on top of a wet cloth. Sprinkle little stuffing mixture on top. Fold the cloth and seal the mixture so that half moon shaped vadai is formed. Deep fry and soak in curds. Serve with garnish II.
   c. **Peas dahi vadai:** Crush fresh peas coarsely. Fry it in little oil till raw smell goes. Add green chilli paste, salt, garam masala, dhania powder, grated fresh coconut and at the end squeeze lime. keep this as a stuffing inside while making vadai. Soak in whipped curds and garnish.

2. **Kachina Thair Vadai:** Whip sour curds. Add little water and dilute it. Grind fresh coconut, little roasted gram, green chillies, jeera, cashewnut, turmeric powder and salt. Mix with whipped curds and boil till raw smell goes. Make medhu vadai and soak it in this for 2 or 3 hours. Serve garnished with coriander leaves.

3. **Ama Vadai:** Soak 1 cup urad and 1 cup thuar dhal together in water for 1 hour. Grind to coarse paste. Deep fry like other vadais. Soak in whipped curds, garnish and serve.

77. BREAD DAHI VADAI

Ingredients:

Bread slices - 12
Milk - ¼ cup.
Salt - as required.
Sugar - ½ tsp.
Fresh thick curds - 1 cup.
Red chilli powder - ½ tsp.
Sweet chutney - 2 Tbl.sps.
(Refer panipuri)
Roasted powdered cumin
   seeds - 1½ tsp.
Chopped coriander
   leaves - 1 Tbl.sp.
Powdered 'Kala namak' - ½ tsp.

Method:

1. Remove brown crusts from bread slices.
2. Sprinkle milk and knead like a dough.
3. Shape like Vadas.
4. Arrange on a plate.
5. Whip curds with salt and sugar.
6. Pour on top of Vadas just before serving.
7. Sprinkle cumin powder, Kala namak, salt, red chilli powder.
8. Garnish with coriander leaves.
9. Put little sweet chutney on top while serving.

Note: This can be made in minutes when unexpected guest arrives. (As there is no need for cooking).

78.   MOONG DHAL PAKODIES

Ingredients:

Green gram dhal - 1 cup.
Oil - for deep frying.
Whipped fresh curds - 1 cup.
Salt & Red chilli
     powder - as required
Dahi masala powder - 1 tsp.
Tomato sauce - as required.

Method:

1. Soak dhal in water for 2 hours.
2. Strain well and grind to frothy paste without adding water.
3. Add salt at the end of grinding.
4. Heat oil in deep curved pan.
5. Using wet hands make small balls from the dough and deep fry till golden.
6. Arrange on a plate.
7. Pour whipped curds on top.
8. Sprinkle salt, red chilli powder, dahi masala powder and tomato sauce. Serve immediately.

Note: Ground paste should be used immediately to make pakodies. Otherwise it looses its frothyness. Do not over stir the batter.

Variations: Soak whole green gram in water for 6 hours. De husk by washing it well. Grind and do the recipe. Plain pakodies can also be served as it is.

Dahi Masala powder: Powder the following ingredients separately and mix together.

        1 tsp. dry ginger.
        1 tsp. black pepper.
        1 tsp. roasted cumin.
        1 tsp. black salt.

79. MYSORE VADAI

Ingredients:

Bengal gram dhal - ½ cup.

Red gram dhal - ½ cup.
(Thuar)

Green gram dhal - ½ cup.

Black gram dhal - ½ cup.
(de husked)

Finely cut cashewnuts and melon
    seeds - 3 Tbl.sps.

Chopped coriander and curry
    leaves - 2 Tbl.sps.

Crushed ginger - 1 tsp.(Optional)

Minced green chillies - 1 Tbl.sp.

Salt - as required.

Oil - for deep frying.

Method:

1. Soak all the dhals together in water for 3 hours.
2. Drain well and grind coarsely with enough salt.
3. Add all the other ingredients.
4. Mix well and make lemon sized balls.
5. Flatten and deep fry in hot oil till crisp and brown on both sides. Serve hot.

To prevent stains inside pressure cooker put squeezed lemon peels at the bottom while cooking.

80. MADHUR VADAI

Ingredients:

Maida - ½ cup.

Rawa - ½ cup.

Rice flour - ½ cup.

Wheat flour - ½ cup.

Finely chopped onions - 1 cup.

Chopped coriander and
curry leaves - 3 Tbl.sps.

Minced green chillies - 1 Tbl.sp.

Salt - as required.

Oil - To deep fry.

Method:

1. Mix all the ingredients together in a bowl.
2. Put 3 Tablespoons of hot oil to that. Blend evenly using finger tips to mix the flour.
3. Divide the flour to six portions.
4. Sprinkle water to first portion to make like a thick dough.
5. Make balls and flatten it on a plastic sheet (or) Plantain leaf to make thin vadai.
6. Deep fry in hot oil till crisp and brown.

Note: Water should be added to the flour each time separately just before deep frying. (As oil holds).

81.   MASAL VADAI

Ingredients:

Bengal gram dhal - 1 cup.

Finely chopped onions - ¼ cup.

Green chillies - 7.

Crushed ginger - 1 tsp.(Optional)

Chopped coriander and
     curry leaves - 2 Tbl.sps.

Salt - as required.

Oil - enough to deep fry.

Method:

1. Soak dhal inwater for 2 hours.
2. Drain water completely and grind to coarse paste.
3. Add salt and other ingredients.
4. Make lemon sized balls, flatten and deep fry in hot oil. (8 to 10 vadais can be deep fried at a time (or) till oil holds).
5. Serve hot with pickle.

Variations:

1. Grind red chillies, cumin seeds, asafoetida and few small onions together. Mix with ground dhal paste. Add drumstick leaves and aniseed. Make vadai as mentioned previously.
2. Finely chopped mint leaves (or) any other greens can be added.
3. ¼ cup of split white peas can be added while soaking for more crisper vadai.

82. GHERUGU VADAI

Ingredients:

Rice flour - 1 cup.

Water - 1 cup.

Ghee - 2 tsps.

Roasted gram powder - 1½ Tbl.sps.
(Chutney gram)

Gingilli seeds - 2 tsps.

Soaked green gram dhal - 2 tsps.

Soaked bengal gram dhal - 2 tsps.

Coarsely crushed peanuts - 1 Tbl.sp.

Salt - as required.

Red chilli powder - ½ tsp.

Chopped coriander curry
leaves - 1 Tbl.sp.

Oil - For deep frying.

To Make:

Rice flour: Soak Rice in water for ½
an hour. Drain well and mill (or)
pound till fine powder. Sieve and dry
under shade for 1 or 2 days. Store in
air tight containers.

Method:

1. Measure water and pour in a heavy bottom deep curved pan.
2. Add salt and ghee.
3. When it starts bubbling up pour flour as a heap in the centre.
4. Switch off the stove and stir briskly.
5. When it becomes bearably warm add melted ghee and other ingredients.
6. Knead to a smooth dough sprinkling more water if necessary.
7. Make lemon sized balls and pat into thin vadai over a plastic sheet.
8. Then put it in hot oil till golden brown and crisp. Serve hot.

Variations:

Omit gram flour, gingilli seeds and peanuts. Use ½ cup maida and ½ cup rice flour. Add chopped onions, coriander and mint leaves. Make vadai as mentioned.

83. MULLANGI VADAI

Ingredients:

White radish - ¼ kg.
(Mullangi)

Salt - as required.

Rice flour - Just enough to hold
the radish.

Oil - for deep frying.

POUND COARSELY:

Green chillies - 7

Chopped coriander
leaves - 2 Tbl.sps.

Salt - a pinch.

Method:-

1. Scrape outer skin from radish and grate it using a fine grater.
2. Add chillies, coriander paste, salt and rice flour to form a stiff dough.
3. Make balls and pat on top of a wet cloth or plastic sheet to form thin vadai.
4. Deep fry few at a time in hot oil till crisp and brown on both sides. Serve hot.

Smear few drops of castor oil to legumes and pulses to prevent pests in it.

84. PULUSU VADAI

Ingredients:

Par boiled rice - 1 cup.
Chopped and cooked.
Red pumpkin pieces - 1 cup.
Red chillies - 10
Tamarind - gooseberry sized.
Salt - as required.
Asafoetida - a pinch.
Chopped curry leaves and
coriander leaves - 2 Tbl.sps.
Soaked bengal gram dhal - 1 Tbl.sp.
Oil - for deep frying.

Method:-

1. Soak rice in warm water for 1½ to 2 hours.
2. Grind it along chillies, cooked pumpkin, tamarind and salt to smooth paste (without adding water).
3. After grinding mix soaked bengal gram dhal, coriander, curry leaves, asafoetida to the dough.
4. Make into lemon sized balls, pat on a plastic sheet to thin vadai and deep fry in hot oil.

Note:

This vadai should be soft to eat. Do not deep fry for longer time. Drain excess oil on a paper and then serve.

Variations:

1. Use ¼ cup of raw rice along with boiled rice while soaking.
2. Instead of pumpkin grind handfull of soaked thuar and 1½ Tbl. sps. grated fresh coconut.
3. Omit pumpkin. Use boiled tapioca pieces and do the recipe.

85. MILAGU VADAI

Ingredients:

Dehusked black gram - 1 cup.
(white urad)
Black pepper - 1 tsp.
Cumin seeds - 1 tsp.
Salt - as required.
Oil - for deep frying.

Method:-

1. Soak dhal in water for 15 minutes.
2. Drain water completely and grind to coarse paste preferably in stone grinder using minimum water possible.
3. Add salt and coarsely powdered pepper, Cumin and 3 tablespoons of hot oil to the dough.
4. Make small balls and pat on a wet cloth to make thin vadai.
5. Make a hole in the centre and deep fry in hot oil.
6. Make all the balls in the same manner and quickly deep fry till half done.
7. When all the vadais are deep fried once again put in hot oil and deep fry till crisp.

Note:

This is made mainly for offering God in Anjaneya temples. If this method is followed correctly gives best results.

Variations:

1. Add little rawa after grinding dhal to get crispy vadai.
2. Whole black gram with skin can also be used in the above recipe. Omit Cumin seeds. Grind pepper along with dhal.
3. Little rice can also be soaked with dhal to get crisper vadai.

86. PERUGU VADAI

Ingredients:

Sour thick curds - 1 cup.
* Rice flour - 1 cup.
(washed, dried and then milled).
Minced green chillies - 2 tsps.
Chopped coriander
leaves - 2 Tbl.sps.
Salt - as required.
Soaked bengal gram
dhal - 1 Tbl.sp.
Oil - for Deep frying.

Method:-

1. Whip curds well and strain it. Dilute with ¼ cup of water.
2. Heat this with salt and a teaspoon of oil in a heavy deep curved pan. (In reduced flame).
3. When it bubbles up put rice flour as a heap in the centre.
4. Switch off the stove and stir briskly with flat laddle.
5. When it cools down to luke warm temperature knead well.
6. Mix soaked dhal, minced chillies and coriander leaves.
7. Make lemon sized balls and flatten into very thin vadai on a plastic sheet.
8. Deep fry in hot oil till it changes its colour. (Cook in reduced flame).

Note:

Do not over fry this. Turn quickly just once and remove from fire. Drain excess oil on absorbant paper (or) on a colander.

87. DRUMSTICK VADAI

Ingredients:

Bengal gram dhal - 1 cup.

Roasted gram - 1 cup.
(chutney dhal)

Drumsticks - 5 (medium sized)

Big onions - 2
(chop finely)

Small onions - 3 or 4

Green chillies - 10 or 12

Garlic - 2 flakes

Ani seeds - ½ tsp.
(Sombu)

Salt - as required.

Oil - to deep fry.

Method:-

1. Soak dhal in water for 2 hours.
2. Cook drumsticks and scoop out the pulp.
3. Grind dhal and roasted gram together to coarse paste.
4. When it is half of done add chillies, small onions, crushed garlic, drumstick pulp and salt.
5. Grind again for few seconds.
6. Add aniseeds, chopped onions and mix well.
7. Prepare vadai as mentioned in previous recipes.

Variation:

Banana flower vadai

Remove yellow stigma from banana flower and chop finely. Steam it in cooker till one whistle sound with salt. Instead of drumstick use this cooked flower in the above recipe.

88. VEGETABLE SANDWICH

Ingredients:

Sliced Bread - 1 loaf.
Butter - 100 gms.
Mint chutney - 3 Tbl sps.
(recipe at the end of this book)
cucumber - 1
carrots - 2
Tomatoes - 2
Green chillies - 6
(Optional)
Onions - 2
Chopped coriander
leaves - 2 Tbl sps.
Salt, pepper powder - as required.

Method:-

1. Remove outer skin and cut the vegetables into thin slices.
2. Mince green chillies and coriander leaves.
3. Trim brown edge crusts of the bread slices with knife or scissors.
4. Apply butter on one side of bread slices.
5. Take one buttered bread slice. Spread little chutney on top of butter.
6. Arrange sliced cucumber and carrots on that.
7. Put one more buttered slice as second layer on top of vegetables. (Butter applied side should face up).
8. Now arrange onions and tomato slices with minced chillies and coriander leaves.
9. Sprinkle salt, pepper with a squeeze of lime on the vegetables.
10. Top with third slice of bread (Butterd side facing down).
11. Press well and cut into four square pieces with sharp knife.
12. Dot with tomato ketchup and serve immediately.

Note:

The chutney should be ground to thick paste with minimum water possible.

89. CLOSED SANDWICHES
(a). CHILLI CHEESE SANDWICH

Ingredients:

Bread slices - 12

Cheese cubes - 3

Pasteurised butter - 100 gms.

Green chillies - 3

Finely cut onions - 3 Tbl. sps.

Salt - little.

Pepper powder - ½ tsp.

Chopped coriander

leaves - 1 Tbl.sp.

Method:-

1. Apply little butter to bread slices.
2. Chop green chillies into thin round pieces.
3. Grate cheese using a fine cheese grater.
4. Mix all the other ingredients together, for filling except bread.
5. Keep little of the filling in between two slices of bread.
6. Press and toast using a sandwhich toaster. (Both sides till brown).
7. Serve with ketchup or mint Chutney.

Variation:

Little worcestershire sauce can be sprinkled to the filling when mixing together.

(b). CARROT SANDWICH

Ingredients:

Carrots - ¼ kg.

Onions - 2

Ginger, green chilli paste - 2 tsps.

Tomatoes - 2

Chopped mint, coriander, curry leaves - 2 Tbl.sps.

Salt - as required.

Oil - for frying.

Bread slices - 10.

Method:-

1. Steam cook carrots and then grate it.
2. Chop onions and tomatoes finely.
3. Heat little oil, and little mustard and then ginger chilli paste.
4. After a minute add onions and fry till crisp.
5. Stir in tomatoes and continue frying till moisture is absorbed.
6. Add grated carrots, salt, chopped leaves and fry well.
7. Keep little masala inbetween two buttered slices of bread. Toast it using sandwich maker.
8. Serve with mint chutney or tomato ketchup.

Note:

After frying this can be ground like a chutney and used as a sandwich spread.

(c). PANEER SANDWICH

Ingredients:

Bread slices - 16

*Paneer - made from 1 litre milk.

Maida - 1 Tbl.sp.

Sprouted green gram - ½ cup.

Tomato sauce - 1½ Tbl.sps.

Salt - as required.

Red chilli powder - 1 tsp.

Garam masala powder - ½ tsp.

Worecestershire sauce - 2 tsps.

Pepper powder - ¼ tsp.

Oil or butter - for applying on
               top of bread.

Method:-

1. Crumble *paneer and mix with maida and other ingredients.
2. Apply butter to bread slices.
3. Use this to sandwich in between two slices of bread and toast using sandwich toaster.

Note:

This can be applied on top of bread slice with grated cheese and diced capsicum. Bake under a grill till cheese melts.

*Paneer - cottage cheese.

(Refer the book 100-vegetarian gravies - Page no. 4)

90. OPEN SANDWICHES
(a). POTATO BREAD SANDWICH

Ingredients:

Potatoes - ¼ kg.

Onions - 2

Green chillies - 6

Pepper powder - ½ tsp.

Red chilli powder - ½ tsp.

Chopped coriander
leaves - 2 Tbl.sps.

Garam masala powder - ¼ tsp.

Bread slices - 8

Butter - 2 tsps.

Dry bread crumbs - 3 Tbl.sps.

Bengal gram flour - 2½ Tbl.sps.

Salt - as required.

Turmeric powder - ¼ tsp.

Oil - for frying.

Method:-

1. Pressure cook potatoes. Peel and mash coarsely.
2. Chop onions and chillies finely.
3. Heat little oil and fry chillies, onions till crisp.
4. Add powdered ingredients and then mashed potatoes.
5. Stir well for few minutes.
6. Remove from fire and mix coriander leaves.
7. Fry bengal gram flour separately in little ghee till good smell comes. (in low flame).
8. Mix with potatoes and apply little of this mixture to one side of buttered bread slice.
9. Dust with fine bread crumbs. Press well with hands.
10. Shallow fry on a hot tawa with enough oil on both sides till crisp.
11. Serve with tomato ketchup.

(b). CORN SANDWICH

Ingredients:

Corn cobs - 3

Bread slices - 10

Finely cut onion - 2 Tbl.sps.

Fresh cream - 2 Tbl.sps. (optional)

Mustard powder - ¼ tsp.

Salt - as required.

Chopped green chillies - 1 Tbl.sp.

Chopped mint leaves - 1 Tbl.sp.

Aji-no-moto - ¼ tsp.

Pepper powder - ½ tsp.

Cheese cubes - 2

Butter - 1 Tbl.sp.

Chopped spring onion
stalks - 2 Tbl.sp.

Method:-

1. Pressure cook corn cobs.
2. Remove the seeds from the cooked cobs.
3. Heat little oil and add cumin seeds, chillies and then onions.
4. Fry for two minutes.
5. Add spring onion stalks, cooked corn, aji-no-moto and stir fry for few minutes.
6. Add salt, pepper, mint leaves, mustard powder and cream.
7. Mix well. Remove from fire.
8. Pile little corn mixture on top of buttered bread slice.
9. Sprinkle little grated cheese and grill till cheese turns its colour. (in an oven).

Add a teaspoon of sugar while cooking cauliflower to prevent discolouring.

---

91. TOASTS
(a). TOMATO TOAST

Ingredients:

Bread slices - 12
Tomatoes - ¼ kg.
(ripe and red)
Finely cut onions - ¼ cup.
Finely chopped coriander
leaves - 2 Tbl.sps.
Sugar - 1 tsp.
Salt - ¾ tsp.
Red chilli powder - ¾ tsp.
Garam masala powder - ¼ tsp.
Oil - for frying.
Ghee - 1 Tbl.sp.

Method:-

1. Apply ghee on both sides of the bread slices.
2. Chop and grind tomatoes to smooth paste. (Do not add water).
3. Strain well to remove seeds and pulp.
4. Mix other ingredients to this juice.
5. Heat a 'tawa' and put a slice of bread on top.
6. After one second turn over.
7. Apply 1 Tbl.sp. of prepared tomato juice on top of the bread slice. spread evenly.
8. Pour little oil around.
9. Turn over and cook again with little more oil, for 1 minute.
10. Serve immediately.

(b). MASALA TOAST

Ingredients:

Bread slices - 10
Butter - 1 Tbl.sp.

Chutney:

Ginger - 1 inch piece.
Garlic - 4 flakes.
Cumin seeds ½ tsp.
Red chilli powder - 1 tsp.
Salt - as required.
roasted gram - 1 Tbl.sp.
(Chutney dhal)
Tamarind - little.
(Grind above ingredients
together to smooth paste)

Method:-

1. Apply butter to bread slices on both sides.
2. Spread little chutney on both sides.
3. Toast on a hot 'Tawa' with (or) without oil on both sides. (as per taste).

Wash flasks with vinegar solution to prevent bad odour in it.

(c). MOONG DHAL TOAST

Ingredients:

Bread slices - 12

Chutney: Grind to fine paste

Green chillies - 6

Coriander leaves - 1 bunch.

Raw mango - little

or

Lemon juice

Cumin seeds - ½ tsp.

Salt - to taste.

Sugar - to taste.

Grind coarsely:

Ani seed - ½ tsp.

Ginger - ½ inch piece.

Green chillies - 4

Red chilli powder - ½ tsp.

Salt - to taste.

Moong dhal - 1 cup.

(Dehusked green gramdhal)

(soaked in water for 2 hrs).

Method:-

1. Apply thin layer of chutney to one side of buttred bread slice.
2. Apply another layer of dhal paste on top.
3. Deep fry in hot oil dhal side downwards first.
4. Turn over gently and fry till golden.
5. Drain off excess oil.
6. Serve hot with tomato ketchup.

Note:

1. Use only day old bread (stale) otherwise bread consumes more oil.
2. This can be toasted on a hot tawa with enough oil on both sides.

92. SANDWICH ROLL

Ingredients:

Bread - 1 loaf
(without slicing)

Mint chutney ⎫ Recipe given at the
Tomato chutney ⎭ end of this book.

Butter - 100 gms

Tomato ketchup

For granishing:

chopped coriander
leaves - 2 Tbl sps

Method:-

1. Buy fresh bread.
2. Put in a polythene (plastic) cover, close properly and keep in freezer compartment of refregirator for ½ hour.
3. Remove and slice it breadthwise (as shown in fig) to long thin slices using bread knife or any sharp knife.

4. Trim the crusts.
5. Flatten each slice with a rolling bin gently.
6. Apply a thin layer of butter on top.
7. Spread little mint chutney.
8. Put one more slice on top as another layer.
9. Apply butter and then tomato chutney.
10. Roll it from one end to the other carefully. (Keep on a damp cloth while doing so)
11. Put in a plastic cover (or) wrap it in a aluminium foil and keep in freezer compartment for ½ hour.
12. Remove and slice into circles. Garnish and serve immediately.

Note:

Instead of doing as rolls, this can be prepared as normal sandwich with three slices applying mint chutney in one layer and tomato chutney to another layer of bread, as tricolour sandwich.

* Tomato chutney - Refer page No -137 in the book 100 Tiffen varieties.

93. ALOO CHAT-I

Ingredients:

Cooked potatoes - ½ kg.

Fresh thick curd - 1 cup.

Chat masala powder - to taste.

Green chutney: (Grind to
                  smooth paste)

Green chillies - 2.

Salt - ½ tsp.

Coriander leaves - 1 bunch.

Sweet and sour sauce:

Tamarind extract - ½ cup.

Dhania powder - 1 Tbl. sp.

Sugar or Jaggery - ¼ cup.

Salt, chilli powder - to taste.

Roasted, powdered cumin
              seeds - 1 tsp.

Chat Masala - Refer page No. 124

Method:

1. Select even sized small potatoes.
2. Peel and slice into two after cooking.
3. Apply little green chutney in between the sliced potato and sandwich together.
4. Whip curd with little salt and sugar.
5. Heat tamarind extract in low flame till raw smell goes.
6. Add salt, jaggery, chilli powder and boil for few more minutes.
7. Just before removing add dhania, Jeera powder.
8. Arrange potatoes on serving dish.
9. Pour sweet and sour sauce over that evenly.
10. Spread curd on top, sprinkle chat masala and serve.

ALOO CHAT-II

Prepare sweet and sour sauce as mentioned in previous recipe. Boil potatoes. Peel and cut into small cubes. Add little salt to fine rawa. Mix with water to knead into thick dough. Pound and knead well. Roll into ¼" thick chappathi. Cut into small diamonds. Deep fry in hot oil till crisp in reduced flame. Add this to cooked potatoes with salt, chilli powder, chat masala, finely cut raw onions, crushed '*sev' and sweet and sour sauce. Mix well, garnish with coriander leaves and serve immediately.

*Sev:

Mix bengal gram flour with salt and ground omam. Add water and knead to stiff dough. Put in greased sev press and squeeze directly in oil with circular motion. Deep fry both sides till crisp. Crush and use as in the recipe.

> A teaspoon of ghee or oil added to thuar dhal while cooking helps the dhal to cook faster.

94. ALOO PAPPAD CHAT

Ingredients:

For Pappads:

Maida - ½ cup.

Wheat flour - ½ cup.

Salt - ¼ tsp.

Jeera powder - ½ tsp.

Oil - for deep frying.

Sweet chutney: Refer Pani puri.

Fresh thick curds - 1 cup.

Boiled potatoes - 2 or 3.

Salt, Chilli powder - as required.

Chat masala powder - 1 tsp.

Powdered 'Kala Namak' - ¼ tsp.

Chopped Coriander
            leaves - 1 Tbl. sp.

Method:

1. Mix maida, wheat flour, salt and knead to a stiff dough using enough water.
2. Keep aside for 10 minutes under wet cloth.
3. Knead well and make thin, small puris from the dough.
4. Deep fry in oil till crisp. (in low flame).
5. Cook potatoes. Peel and dice into even cubes.
6. Arrange pappads on a plate.
7. Spread potatoes over them.
8. Spread whipped curds as next layer.
9. Sprinkle salt, chilli powder, chat masala, 'Kala Namak' and chopped coriander leaves on top of that.

95. MATTAR CHAT

Ingredients:

Fresh Green peas - 2 cups.

Cumin seeds - ½ tsp.

Green chillies - 3.

Salt - as required.

Roasted, powdered cumin - ¼ tsp.

Pepper, powder - ¼ tsp.

Powdered 'Kala Namak' - ½ tsp.

Oil - 1 Tbl. sp.

Chat masala powder - ½ tsp.

Dried, powdered mint - 1 tsp.

Chopped coriander
              leaves - 1 Tbl. sp.

Whipped fresh curds - ½ cup.

Coarsely crushed puri
              pieces - ¼ cup.
(from pani puri)

Chopped onions - ¼ cup.

Sweet chutney - 1 Tbl. sp.

*Sev - ¼ cup. (Refer Aloo Chat).

Method:

1. Heat little oil and add cumin seeds, slit green chillies.
2. Reduce heat and put fresh peas.
3. Sprinkle water and cover with a lid.
4. When peas are tender and moisture is absorbed add all the dry powders.
5. Mix well and remove from fire.
6. Arrange on a serving dish.
7. Sprinkle crushed puri pieces, onions, whipped thick curds and top with sweet chutney and *Sev.
8. Serve immediately.

114

96. FRUIT AND VEGETABLE CHAT

Ingredients:

Firm ripe Bananas - 2 or 3.
Orange - 1 or 2.
(ripe, sweet).
Tomatoes - 2.
Boiled potatoes - 2.
Ripe guava (or) Mango - 1.
Lemon - 2.
Coriander leaves - 1 Tbl. sp.
Salt, pepper powder - as per taste.
Chat masala powder - as per taste.

Method:

1. Peel and cut all the vegetables and fruits into even sized pieces.
2. Add salt, lemon juice, chat masala and shake gently to mix.
3. Chill for half an hour.
4. Pile on a serving dish.
5. Dot with fresh cream and serve.

97. FINGER CHIPS

Ingredients:

Potatoes - ½ kg.
Salt - as required.
Pepper powder (or)
Red chilli powder - 1 tsp.
Oil - for frying.

Method:

1. Scrape outer skin from potatoes and cut them into even sized finger like pieces.
2. Put into salted water.
3. Wash once or twice.
4. Spread over a towel to remove excess moisture.
5. Deep fry in hot oil till golden colour.
6. Remove from fire and drain excess oil.
7. Sprinkle with salt and pepper.
8. Serve hot with tomato ketchup.

98. CRISP GROUNDNUTS

Ingredients:

Dehusked groundnuts - 2 cups.
(dry)
Garlic - 1 flake.
Salt, chilli powder - to taste.
Oil - to deep fry.

Method:

1. Heat water in a broad pan.
2. When it starts boiling put crushed garlic and groundnuts.
3. Bring to boil once again.
4. Remove from fire and keep closed for 5 to 10 minutes.
5. Drain on a colander to remove water.
6. Fold a thick towel. Spread groundnuts inbetween the foldings.
7. Wipe well and press with palms to remove the red husk. (Peel off the red husk completely.)
8. Deep fry in hot oil using a wire frying basket.
9. Drain excess oil and sprinkle salt and chilli powder when it is still hot.

<u>Note</u>: When groundnuts are fried in this manner it gets a shine and tastes good.

Variations:

Masala Groundnuts:

Mix bengal gram flour, salt, chilli powder, garam masala with very little water. Coat on groundnuts. Deep fry by crumbling and putting directly in hot oil.

99.   POP CORN

Ingredients:

Dry corn seeds - ¼ cup.
Powdered salt - ¼ tsp.
Powdered kala namak - little.
Black pepper powder - ¼ tsp.
Garam masala powder - ¼ tsp.
Oil - 2 Tbl. Sps.
Turmeric powder - a pinch.

Method:

1. Heat a deep curved broad *'kadai' with oil.
2. When it smokes reduce flame and put all the powders and corn in the oil.
3. Close with a proper big lid so that when corn pops with splutters, it will not spill over.
4. When the spluttering stops take the lid out and switch off the stove.
5. Serve immediately or store in air tight container.

Note:

Do not put more corn at one time. A handfull to ¼ cup itself makes a 'kadai'full of pop corn.

*Kadai – Deep curved frying pan.

100.   INSTANT BHEL - I

Ingredients:

Puffed rice - 5 cups.
(Pori)
Finely cut onions - 2 Tbl. sps.
Roasted gram - 2 Tbl. sps.
Oil - 1½ Tbl. sp.
Salt - as required.
Red chilli powder - ¾ tsp.
Chopped coriander
           leaves - 1 Tbl. sp.
Finely cut green mango
           pieces - 1½ Tbl. sp.
Finely cut tomatoes - 1 Tbl. sp.
Grated carrots - 2 Tbl. sps.
Grated beet root - 2 Tbl. sps.
Lemon - 1.

Method:

1. Mix puffed rice and roasted gram in a bowl.
2. Sprinkle oil and coat well on puffed rice using hands.
3. Add salt, chilli powder and mix well.
4. Mix other ingredients quickly with lemon juice to the puffed rice.
5. Serve immediately.

To remove kerosine smell from hands apply little curds and then wash well.

INSTANT BHEL - II

Ingredients:

Puffed rice - 4 cups.
Oil - 1 Tbl. sp.
Roasted gram - 1 Tbl. sp.
Roasted peanuts - 1 Tbl. sp.
Small onion - ¼ cup.
Lemon - 1 small.
Salt - to taste.
Red chilli powder - ½ tsp.

For Green Chutney:

Grated fresh coconut - ¼ cup.
Green chillies - 3.
Coriander leaves - ½ bunch.
Chutney gram - 1 tsp.
Salt - little.

Method:

1. Peel and slice small onions.
2. Soak in lime juice with salt and chilli powder for one hour.
3. Grind chutney with minimum water possible and keep in a refrigerator for ½ an hour.
4. Mix peanuts and gram with puffed rice in a bowl.
5. Add 1 Tbl. sp. oil and smear well with hands.
6. Add chutney, soaked onion with the lime juice, salt and chilli powder.
7. Mix well and serve immediately.

MINT CHUTNIES FOR CUTLETS

1.

Ingredients:

Mint leaves - 2 cups.
Coriander leaves - 1 cup.
Green chillies - 6.
Grated fresh Coconut - 1 Tbl. sp.
Onion - 1.
Salt - as required.
Oil - 1 tsp.

Method:

1. Heat oil and fry green chillies, mint and coriander leaves.
2. Add salt, onion, coconut and grind to smooth paste.
3. Serve with cutlets.

2.

Ingredients:

Green chillies - 7.
Small onions - 10.
Dhania - 1 tsp.
Mint leaves - 1½ cups.
Grated fresh coconut - 1½ Tbl. sps.
Salt - as required.
Tamarind - small gooseberry sized.
Oil - 1 Tbl. sp.

For seasoning:

Mustard seeds - ¼ tsp.
Bengal gram dhal - 1 tsp.
Asafoetida - a pinch.

Method:

1. Heat little oil and fry chillies, dhania, small onions, mint leaves, one by one.
2. Add coconut at the end and remove from fire.
3. Add salt, tamarind and grind to smooth paste.
4. Heat little oil and add seasonings.
5. Pour on top of chutney and mix well.

3.

Ingredients:

Mint leaves - 1½ cup.
Onion -1.
Green chillies - 6.
Ginger - 1 inch piece.
Tamarind - little.
Anardhana - 2 tsps.
(Dry pomogranate seeds)
Salt - as required.
Oil & mustard seeds - for tampering.

Method:

1. Grind all the ingredients to smooth paste. (with very minimum water).
2. Tamper mustard seeds in hot oil and pour on top.
3. Use as sandwich spread.

Variation:

Coriander leaves and mint leaves can be mixed equally in the above chutney.

CHUTNIES AS SANDWICH SPREADS

1. CORIANDER CHUTNEY

Ingredients:

Chopped coriander leaves - 1 cup.
Curry leaves - ½ cup.
Red chillies - 5.
Tomatoes - 2.
Tamarind - Gooseberry sized
soak in water).
Salt - as required.
Oil - 1 Tbl. sp.

For tampering:

Oil - 1 tsp.
Mustard seeds - ¼ tsp.

Method:

1. Heat little oil and fry red chillies, tomatoes and then chopped coriander, curry leaves.
2. Grind with tamarind and salt.
3. Heat oil and tamper with mustard seeds.
4. Pour on top of chutney and mix well.
5. Use this chutney as a sandwich spread.

2.   GARLIC CHUTNEY

Ingredients:

Garlic - 25 flakes.
Red chillies - 10.
Cumin seed (Jeera) - 1 tsp.
Tamarind - gooseberry sized.
Salt - as required.
Curry leaves - ¼ cup.

For seasoning:

Oil - 1 tsp.
Mustard - ¼ tsp.

Method:

1. Fry red chillies, curry leaves, garlic and cumin seed in little oil.
2. Grind with salt and soaked tamarind to smooth paste.
3. Heat oil and add mustard seeds to crackle.
4. Mix with chutney.
5. Use as a sandwich spread on buttered toast.

3.   COCONUT CHUTNEY

Ingredients:

Grated fresh coconut - ¼ cup.
Ginger - 1 inch piece.
Red chillies - 10.
Onion - 1.
(dice into medium pieces).
Tamarind - little.
Salt - as required.

Method:

Grind all the ingredients to coarse paste. Heat little oil and tamper mustard seeds, pour on top. Mix well and use as sandwich spread (or) serve with idli, dosa etc.

4. MINT CHUTNEY FOR SANDWICH

Ingredients:

Mint leaves - 1 cup.
Ginger - ½ inch piece.
Garlic - 2 flakes.
Green chillies - 4.
Onion - 1.
Chopped green mango - 1 Tbl. sp.
(or) Lime juice - 1 Tbl. sp.
Salt - as required.

Method:

1. Grind everything to smooth paste.
2. Use as a sandwich spread.

CHAT MASALA POWDER

Ingredients:

Red chillies - ½ cup.
Dhania (coriander seeds) - ¼ cup.
Rock salt (powder
            separately) - ¼ cup.
Kala Namak - 2 Tbl. sps.
Dry Mango powder - 4 Tbl. sps.
                        (heaped)
                Or
Pomegranate seeds.
Cardamom - 15.
Cinnamon - 10 pieces.
Cloves - 15.
Black pepper - 1 Tbl. sp.

Method:

1. Dry red chillies, dhania and garam masala spices under hot sun.
2. Pound to fine powder and mix other ingredients.
3. Use as required in the recipe.
(Powdered dry mint leaves can also be included if liked).

TOMATO KETCHUP

Ingredients:

Tomatoes - 1 kg.
Salt - 1½ Tbl. sp.
Sugar - 2 Tbl. sps.
White Vinegar - ½ cup.
K.M.S. powder - ¼ tsp.

For spice bag: (Pound Coarsely)

Cinnamon - 3 pieces (1 inch).
Cloves - 4.
Cardamom - 4.
Garlic - 4 flakes.
Small onions - 6.
(or)
Big onion - ½.
Cumin seeds - ½ tsp.
Whole pepper - ½ tsp.
Green chillies - 3.

Method:

1. Select firm, ripe, red tomatoes.
2. Discard green portions if any.
3. Heat water in a broad vessel.
4. When it starts boiling add whole tomatoes to immerse in it.
5. Bring to boil once again.
6. Remove from fire and keep closed for few minutes.
7. Strain water and peel outer skin from tomatoes.
8. Grind to smooth pulp and strain to remove any seeds.
9. Pound the ingredients given for spice bag coarsely.
10. Tie in a thin muslin cloth and put into tomato pulp.
11. Boil in medium flame, stirring occasionally till the pulp reduces to ⅓ of its consistency.
12. Add salt and sugar. Mix well and remove from fire.
13. Add vinegar and K.M.S. powder.
14. Squeeze out the spice bag carefully and remove with a tongs (or) laddle. (Do not use hands for squeezing).
15. Pour in clean sterilized bottles.

OUR BOOKS ARE SOLD AT :

At BANGALORE:
VASAN BOOK DEPOT
1st Cross, Gandhi Nagar.

T.N.KRISHNIAH SETTY & SON
234, Chickpet, Bangalore:53

GANGARAMS
72, M.G.Road, Bangalore: 1

SAPNA BOOK HOUSE
(Opp: Tribhuvan theatre)
Gandhi nagar. Bangalore:9.

IIIGGINBOTHAMS LTD
68, M.G.Road, Bangalore:1.

SUBHAS STORES
72, Avenue Road, Bangalore:2

NILGIRIS
171, Brigade Road.

PRISM - THE BOOK SHOP
16, 11th Main, 4th Block
Jaya Nagar, Banglore:11

AT MYSORE:
Geetha Book House
K.R.Circle, Mysore:1

Parimalamma
235, 12h Main Road
Saraswathipuram, Mysore:9

At VILLIPURAM
CHARUKRISHNA
3, Kubera street, Villipuram:1

AT KANCHIPURAM:
JOTHI STORE
110, Gandhi Raod.

AT PONDICHERY:
Higginbothams Ltd
34, Ambour Salai, Pondichery.

AT CUDDALORE:
BELL BOOK HOUSE
4, Imperial Road, Cuddalore:2

AT ERODE:
NILIGIRIS DAIRY FARM
LTD, Sampath Nagar.

SANGEETHA SHOPING
24, Sivashanmugam st,
Erode:1

AT TRICHY:
VEE PEE AGENCIES
168, Periar Nagar
T V Koil, Trichy. Ph:2434391

AGASTHIAR BOOK DEPOT
9A, Clives Bldg, Nandhi koil st
Trichy:2

BHARATH BOOK HOUSE
16, 1st Cross, Thillai nagar,
Trichy:2

RASI PUBLICATIONS
2, Tamil Sangam Bldg,
46-A, W.B.Road, Trichy : 8

Nilgiris - Trichy

At PALANI:
KALAIMAGAL STORES
337, Gandhi Road, Palani:1

AT SALEM:
Mrs. B.SUMATHI
1-C/1, Rajaji Road. Salem:7.
Phone:415400

CHANDRA BOOK SHOP
No.5, Car Street.

SAI GIRIDHAR STORES
Opp:Sarada College, Fair lands.

BHARATHI SUPER
MARKET- Hasthampatti.

Nilgiris - Salem

At NAMAKKAL:
Namakkal Super Market'
9, Thuraiyur Road.

AT KARUR:
SRI VANI BOOK SHOP
CNKK Complex,
176-A, Jawahar bazar, Karur-1

AT COIMBATORE:
CHERAN BOOK HOUSE
137, Big Bazaar Street,
Coimbatore-1

MANNA BOOK HOUSE
Lakshmi Complex, .
Cross cut Rd, Gandhipuram.

VIJAYA PATHIPPAKAM
20, Raja street, Coimbatore:1

Nilgiris Dept stores
739-A, Avinashi Road.

KANDASAMY PATHIPPAKAM
9, Peoples Park, Combtr:18

ANVESHANA
Lakshmi Plaza Combines
1089, Avinashi Rd,
Coimbatore:37

RADHAMANI STORES
137, Raja St, Coimbatore:1

Kannan Dept Stores
130, Rajaji st, Coimbatore:9

AT MAYILADUTHURAI:
ZAM ZAM SUPER MARKET
Mahadhana St

AT KRISHNAGIRI:
Mrs.C.BARATHI
D-14, 2nd Cross,
Co-op Colony Road.

AT HOSUR:
INDIAN BOOK CENTRE
11/7, Ramar koil st.

AT MADURAI:
SELVI BOOK SHOP
151-A, Netaji Road, Madurai:1.

BOOK PLAZA
18, Town Hall Road, Madurai:1

MANO BOOK CENTRE
155, Pudh Mandapam,
Madurai:1

MEENAKSHI BOOK SHOP
Shivalingam Towers
99-B East Avani Mula st,
Madurai:1

Higginbothams Ltd

At TUTICORIN
SUMANGALI SUPER MARKET
239, North Car St, Tuticorin:2

At KUMBAKONAM:
Sri Markandeya Book Depot
48, Kumbeswarr Sannidhi.

At TIRUNELVELI:
Sri Shyamala Puthaga Nilayam
50, T.M.Building, Tirunelveli J

At MANGALORE:
SCHOOL BOOK CO
Car st, Mangalore:1

At TIRUVANNAMALAI
SARASWATHI STORES
40, Car street, R M Building.

At POLLACHI:
PINKY READY MADE JUNCTION
86/2, Udumalpet Road

At BOMBAY:
GIRI TRADING AGENCY
Opp: Post Office, Matunga,
Bombay: 19

At U S A: Buy books on-line.
Visit innoconcepts.com

<u>Note:</u> Please Send Demand drft in Advance with extra charge of Rs.20/- for each order of maximum
4 books. We will send Books by COURIER

OUR BOOKS ARE SOLD IN CHENNAI AT :

PRADEEP ENTERPRISES, 20,Poes Garden,Chennai:86.

HIGGINBOTHAMS LTD
814,Anna Salai. Chennai:2.

NILGIRIS
58, Dr Radhakrishna Road
Chennai:4

KALAIMAGAL TRADERS
7, Ponnambala Vadhiyar St,
Mylapore, Chennai:4

KARTHIK BOOK SHOP
30,South Mada st
Mylapore, Chennai: 4

VIJAYA STORES
24/1,South Mada Street,
Mylapore. Chennai: 4.

Giri Trading Co
10,Kapaleswarar Sannidhi
Mylapore.

Vijaya Shopee
51,R.K.Mutt Road,
Mylapore.

**MAHARAJA SHOPPING
PLAZA**
113-A, Poonamallee High
Road, Chennai: 10

Nilgiris -Chetpet
879, P.II Road (Next to
Ega)

SAKTHI BOOK CENTRE
40/99,Sir Thyagaraya Rd
Pondy Bazar, T.Nafar

NEW BOOK LAND
52,North Usman Road,
T.Nagar

MADRAS BOOK HOUSE
4,Ranganathan st, T.Nagar.

LIFESTYLE SUPER MRKT
10, S.P. Road, Adyar.

ODYSSEY
15, First Main Road,
Gandhinagar, Adyar.

Nilgiris
Annai Velankani Church Rd
Besant Nagar.

WORDS & WORTHS
26,Second Avenue,
Besant Nagar

SINGAPORE SHOPEE
40/1,East Mada st,Valmiki
Nagar, Thiruvanmayur.

CONNEXIONS
W-122,3rd Avenue,
Annanagar

Vijaya Shopee
SBOA School Road,
Annanagar West Extn

Nilgiris
2nd Avenue, Anna Nagar.

YESEIS SUPER MARKET
T-101, Anna Nagar

Murugan Super Markt
1035, E V High Road,
Arumbakam

SHOPPING SINGAPORE
Main Bazaar,
CollectorNagar,
Mogappair, Chennai:50.

PURCHASE POINT
M.L.M.Complex,
Mahalingapuram.

C L S Book Shop
68, Evening Bazar,
Chennai : 3

BOOK PALACE
12, Pycrofts Road,
Triplicane.

SUDHA STORES
54,Big Street, Triplicane.

**FRIENDS OFFSET
CALENDAR**
39, Bunder street,
Chennai:1

M.K.STORES
40, Bunder st, Chennai:1

FIVE STAR SELECT
24,1st Avenue,Ashok
Nagar.

PRIMAH ENTERPRISES
253, Alagiri samy salai
(Opp:PSBB School)
K.K.Nagar.

SHOPPING SINGAPORE
348,T.H.Road,
Washermanpet

SINGAPORE 2000
105,Paper Mills Road,
Perambur.

SINGAPORE PLAZA
62/1, Arcot Road,
Saligramam

A.R.ENTERPRISES
35,Arcot Road,
Kodambakkam.

Nilgiris
321,Arcot Road, Doshi Garden
Vadapalani

Vijaya Shopee
87/165, Arcot Road
Vadapalani

CONNEXIONS
48,Arcot Road
Saligramam, Chennai.

S & S CONNECTIONS
G-1,Raja Annamalaipuram
2nd Main Road, (OPP: Chennai
KaliappaHospital)

FOOD CITY
7, C.P.Ramasamy Road
Alwarpet, Chennai:18

FIVE STAR CLASSIC
Near R H Hospital
Tiruvanmayur

SINGAPORE SHOPEE
7/18, Indira Gandhi Road
PALLAVARAM

PANDIAN SUPER MARKET
82, Arcot Road
Virugambakkam

Food Marvel
55, Trunk Road
(Opp: Hotel Road) Porur

PONNU SUPER MARKET
Near Rathi Theatre
Ambattur

LAND MARK
Nungambakam High Road,
SPENCERS SHOPPING MALL
Citi Centre- Dr R.K. Road

<u>Note:</u> Please Send Demand drft in Advance with extra charge of Rs.30/- for each order of maximum
4 books. We will send Books by COURIER.